HOW TO HANDLE PROBLEM BEHAVIORS IN SCHOOL

A Manual of Procedures for
Dealing with Problems
Most Frequently Faced
by Elementary School Personnel

By
Marvin Silverman, Ed.D.

pro·ed

5341 Industrial Oaks Blvd.
Austin, Texas 78733

Copyright © 1980 by PRO-ED, Inc.

All rights reserved. No part of this book
may be reproduced in any form or by any means
without prior written permission of the publisher.

Printed in the United States of America

pro-ed

5341 Industrial Oaks Boulevard
Austin, Texas 78735

10 9 8 7 6 5 4 3 2   86 87 88 89 90

Contents

Chapter 1   INTRODUCTION 1
What's it all about?

Chapter 2   CORPORAL PUNISHMENT 3
How effective is corporal punishment in the schools?

Chapter 3   IGNORING AND PRAISING BEHAVIOR 5
What are some effective ways of ignoring inappropriate behavior and praising appropriate behavior?

Chapter 4   IMPROVING BEHAVIOR AND MOTIVATION 11
How can I help a student improve his or her behavior and increase his or her motivation to do his or her work?

Chapter 5   CONFLICT AVOIDANCE 25
How can I teach children alternatives to violence for solving conflicts?

Chapter 6   IMPROVING SCHOOL ATTENDANCE ... 29
How can I help improve children's attendance at school?

Chapter 7   LYING AND TATTLING 35
How can I help reduce children's lying and tattling?

Chapter 8   SCHOOL PHOBIA 39
What can I do to help a child who is afraid to come to school?

Chapter 9   IMPROVING CAFETERIA BEHAVIOR ... 43
How can I help children improve their behavior in the school cafeteria?

Chapter 10   SHY AND NON-ASSERTIVE CHILDREN 49
How can I help the shy and non-assertive child?

Chapter 11	MANNERS AND RESPECT FOR OTHERS	53
	How can I teach children good manners and respect for others?	
Chapter 12	HYPERACTIVE CHILDREN	57
	What can I do to help a hyperactive child adjust to a regular class?	
Chapter 13	AFTER-SCHOOL GUIDANCE ACTIVITIES	61
	My school wants to have an after-school hours guidance activities program. How can we do this?	
Chapter 14	IMPROVING STANDARDIZED TEST PERFORMANCE	69
	How can I help children improve their standardized test performance?	
Chapter 15	LITTLE TECHNIQUES THAT WORK	77
	Tell me about some other ideas for improving life at my school.	
Chapter 16	SUGGESTED READINGS	87
	Well, you answered a lot of my questions, now what?	

to
Howard Goldberg and Michael Tuttle

Two fantastic kids whose friendship with me helped stimulate my desire to share the techniques in this manual with other educators.

Acknowledgments

The author wishes to thank the following for their support and encouragement in the preparation of this manual: Drs. Joan Gelormino, Richard Goldman, and Polly Ebbs of Nova University, Fort Lauderdale, Florida; Dr. Richard Schaeffer, Chairman of the psychology department of Barry College, Miami, Florida; the multitude of teachers in the Dade and Broward County school systems, Florida, who read and reacted to the manuscript; Debbie and Barry Dolin, Dr. Shirley Freeman, Gary Rito, Doris Brand, and the scores of teachers who have implemented many of the techniques suggested in this manual in their classrooms.

Marvin Silverman, Ed.D.
Miami, Florida
1980

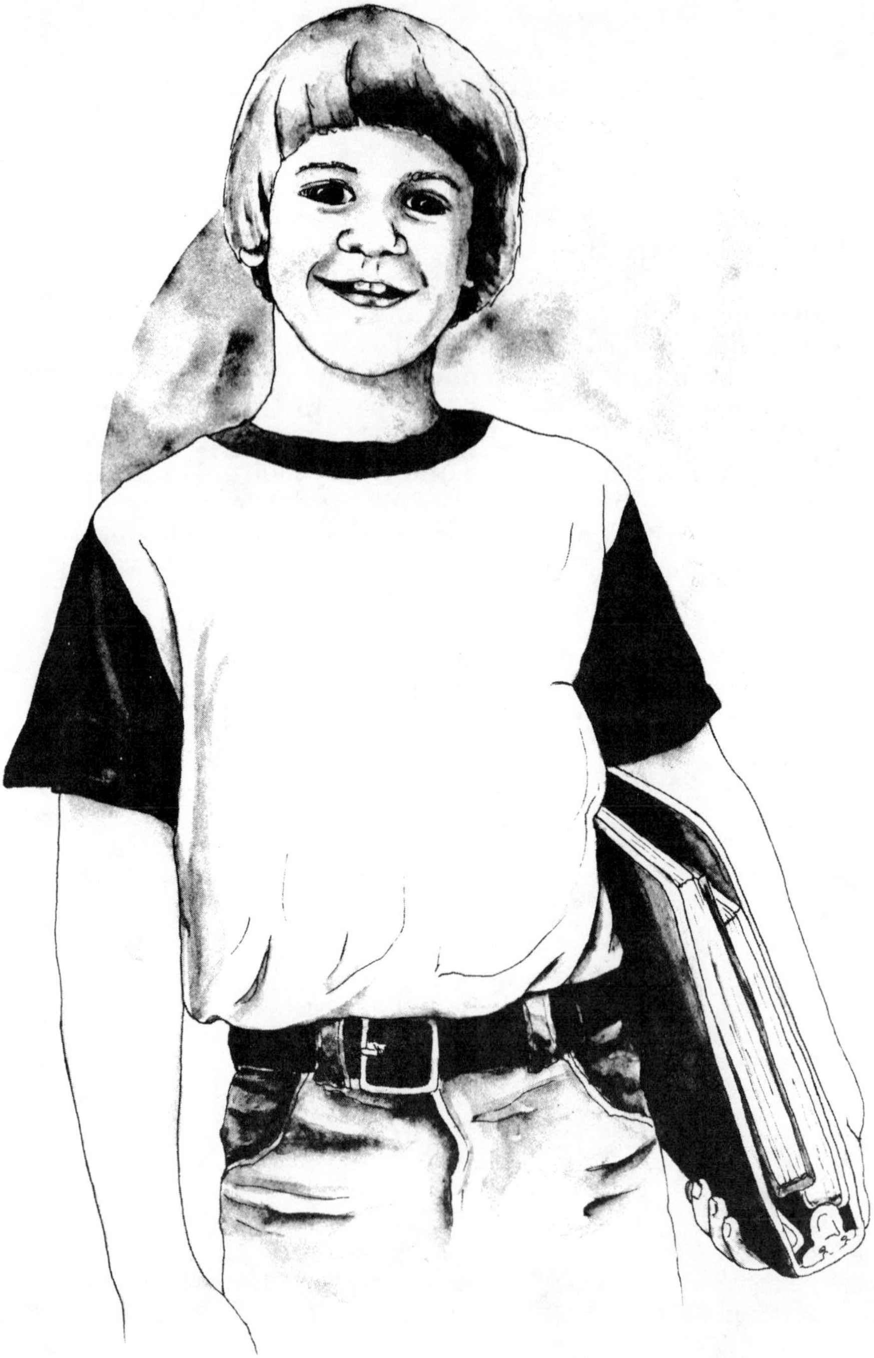

Chapter 1

Introduction

What's it all About?

It's about kids and techniques for improving their school behavior and motivation. This is a how-to manual. Behavior modification theory is not discussed. You can read one of a multitude of books published on this subject if you're interested in theory. This manual tells you how to use behavior modification procedures with elementary school students, classes, and the entire school. Technical jargon is not used.

The terms *behavior management* and *behavior modification* are used synonymously in this manual. You may be thinking to yourself, "What is behavior management?" Behavior management is the teaching of desirable behaviors and the elimination of undesirable behaviors through an organized and systematic application of the methods and experimental findings of behavioral psychology. It is not a theory. It is a science based on research findings. A behavior management program is ineffective unless it is carefully planned and implemented in a consistent manner.

Behavior Management is . . . . .

1. Specifying a behavioral goal to be reached by the child. The teacher reinforces (rewards) gradual successes toward meeting the goal. For example, if the goal is "respect others," a gradual success toward meeting that goal could be "do not tease other kids." The child should be expected to master behaviors one at a time until a whole new set of behaviors is learned.

2. Identifying what is rewarding a bad behavior, withdrawing that reward, and rewarding good behavior.
3. Presenting a punishment or reward immediately after the behavior is exhibited.
4. When a child is improving, much immediate reinforcement (reward) is provided at first and the reinforcement is gradually reduced.
5. Selecting a reinforcer that is meaningful to the child (verbal praise, material reward).
6. Using modeling. Teachers should praise appropriate behaviors exhibited by one child to set an example for the other children. "John, you said 'thank you' after I gave you the book. That's great!"
7. With the child, writing down specific behaviors you expect, e.g., "Talk at the proper time." Define "proper time" for the child. State the consequences for doing and not doing this behavior. Follow the plan.
8. Never using threats! Follow through on any promises you make!

Behavior Management is Not . . . . .

1. Taking good behavior for granted and never recognizing it.
2. Punishing the child by allowing him or her to do something he or she likes (e.g., wash the chalkboard, sit outside the classroom).
3. Putting your arm around a child and saying, "You're so angry today" right after he or she hit another child. This rewards him or her for the aggressive action.
4. Constantly telling a child to raise his or her hand to answer a question and, when he or she does raise it, not verbally recognizing this behavior.
5. Constantly telling a child to take his or her thumb out of his or her mouth and when the thumb is finally out, not saying anything.
6. Using a behavior chart on Monday, forgetting about it on Tuesday, then using it again on Wednesday.

This manual gives you many constructive alternatives to corporal punishment. The next chapter is the only discussion chapter in the manual. It is included because you should know why corporal punishment is not the only answer for dealing with behavior. This knowledge will encourage you to use some of the procedures outlined here.

Chapter 2

Corporal Punishment

How Effective is Corporal Punishment in the Schools?

Research has shown that corporal punishment is destructive and has no positive effects. Then why do some school systems still use corporal punishment? Because there is a gap between research and practice. Although the professional literature does not substantiate corporal punishment as an effective disciplinary technique, the research is ignored by many professionals who are not aware of the literature or who do not accept the research.

Corporal punishment is easy to use. It doesn't require any special training or knowledge. It doesn't require a significant investment of time. It has an immediate effect because it temporarily stops the misbehavior. Studies have shown that corporal punishment temporarily suppresses misbehavior, but the misbehavior will reappear later. That's why we usually see the same kids being spanked again and again. It didn't work last time and it won't work this time. Corporal punishment does not teach the child alternative behaviors. It does teach the child that violence is an acceptable technique for dealing with problems. The child learns that *when adults have a problem with me they hit me. Therefore, hitting is a good thing to do to solve problems.*

Let's take a brief look about what research tells us about corporal punishment.

1. Corporal punishment creates nervousness and tension. Nervousness and tension cause slow learning.
2. People must first interact before they can influence one another. Corporal punishment does not allow for positive interaction.

3. Frequent use of corporal punishment is strongly associated with developing a low self-image in children.
4. Corporal punishment does not teach children constructive ways to resolve conflicts. It actually teaches children that violence is the way to deal with problems.
5. When an adult hits a child, the adult is actually modeling violence for the child.

Amazing! But some educators with college and graduate training still use corporal punishment to solve a problem. This manual provides many alternatives to corporal punishment. These alternatives, although more time consuming than corporal punishment, teach positive behaviors, not violence.

Chapter 3

Ignoring and Praising Behavior

What are Some Effective Ways of Ignoring Inappropriate Behavior and Praising Appropriate Behavior?

"Ignore a bad behavior" is easier said than done. Many teachers start ignoring a child's inappropriate behavior, notice the behavior is getting worse, and resume paying attention to it. That is a poor technique. There are many other techniques to use in ignoring a behavior, and if these techniques are not used carefully, the child's behavior can actually get worse. Let's see how this can occur.

Tony is the class clown. He is constantly making noises to disrupt the class. It's the fourth month that Tony is in Mrs. Bradley's class. Whenever Tony acts up, Mrs. Bradley says, "Tony, stop that!" or takes action, "Tony, sit in the corner." Sometimes Mrs. Bradley's face turns red and she becomes very upset. How great this is for eight-year-old Tony! "Imagine," Tony says to himself, "I'm only eight years old and I have so much power over this teacher! I can make her shake, I can make her yell, and I can make her excited. Wow, this is fun!"

One day, Mrs. Bradley decides she will completely ignore Tony's misbehavior. The first two times Tony acts up, she ignores him. Then, during a math lesson, Tony starts making a noise like a chicken. Mrs. Bradley ignores this but the chicken gets louder and louder. She still ignores it but now Tony is roaming around the room dancing like a chicken and getting louder and louder. Mrs. Bradley decides that ignoring this behavior just isn't working. Finally she yells, "Tony, sit down, I can't stand that noise!" Tony smiles, returns to his seat, and is more disruptive than usual for the rest of the day.

Mrs. Bradley's attempt to extinguish Tony's disruptive behavior by ignoring it failed because she did not follow the principles of ignoring. She actually helped make his behavior worse because she taught him that now, in order to get her attention, he has to be super bad, not just a little bad.

Principles of Ignoring Inappropriate Behavior

1. *Select the specific behavior you want to eliminate.* Focus in on just one behavior. In Tony's case, you could focus on "calling out in class." When this behavior has been eliminated, you can then work on other behaviors.
2. *Ignoring usually does not have an immediate effect.* Be patient. It took years for the child to learn the inappropriate behavior. Don't expect to eliminate it in one day.
3. *When you ignore a behavior, always reinforce an opposite behavior.* Since Mrs. Bradley was trying to ignore Tony's calling out, she should reinforce Tony's not calling out. If Tony is in his seat quietly for even 30 seconds, Mrs. Bradley should say, "Tony, thank you for being quiet for a while. Because you were quiet, you may be the board monitor this morning." Whenever you ignore a behavior, you must always find an opposite good behavior to praise.
Example of Inappropriate Behavior: Hitting
Example of an opposite good behavior: Keeping your hands to yourself.
In these examples, if you want to eliminate a child's hitting behavior, you must reinforce him or her when he or she is not hitting someone.
4. *When you start ignoring a behavior, it may get worse before it gets better.* This is the rule that many teachers are not aware of and not understanding it may lead to failure in the teacher's ignoring attempt. Since the child has been accustomed to getting attention for the behavior, it is quite frustrating when suddenly no attention is given. This frustration often results in a child becoming aggressive and more intense in efforts to get attention. So when the behavior gets worse, a teacher might conclude that the ignoring isn't working and that "I must respond to this behavior." By responding to the behavior, the teacher shows the child that he or she now has to be super bad to get the teacher's attention. Also, it is now more difficult to eliminate because the child has learned that "even though the teacher sometimes ignores me. I

can get her attention eventually if I keep acting up." Once you decide to ignore a behavior, carry it through! If you pay attention to that behavior, even once, *you* have actually strengthened the inappropriate behavior.
5. *Sometimes the behavior you have been ignoring will reappear.* Occasionally, a behavior that has been decreased for some time suddenly reappears. This might be the child's final attempt to be the winner. Once again, ignore the inappropriate behavior to make certain that the child receives no payoff (attention) for the behavior.

Many undesirable behaviors can be decreased by ignoring them if you follow the guidelines above. If you deviate from these guidelines, you can expect your efforts to fail.

ALWAYS REMEMBER THAT WHEN YOU START TO IGNORE A BEHAVIOR, IT PROBABLY WILL GET WORSE AT FIRST AS THE CHILD ATTEMPTS TO TEST YOUR PATIENCE.

Many behaviors that will not lead to physical harm and danger can be ignored. Typical behaviors for which ignoring would be appropriate include:

- Bad words
- Clowning around
- Being a pest
- Talking out
- Frequently leaving seat
- Making noises

Maybe I can ignore a child's behavior but what if the other children in the class pay attention to it?

You can reinforce children for ignoring another child's inappropriate behavior. When Tony is making noises you can say, "Douglas, while someone in the class (Don't give Tony the pleasure of hearing his name) was making noises, you ignored him! Go put your name on the good worker's list on the board." *Teach* your class to ignore inappropriate behaviors and you'll be successful in decreasing such behaviors.

Praising Appropriate Behaviors

We've talked quite a bit about praising appropriate behaviors, and here's how to do it.

1. Praise a good behavior immediately. Immediate reinforcement is very effective. As soon as you see a good behavior, praise it.
2. When you're helping a child learn to exhibit a good behavior, praise that behavior each time it occurs. Later on you can praise it less frequently (e.g., every third time it occurs).
3. Praise Improvements. Never expect 100% improvement immediately. So when Tony calls out only once in five minutes instead of his usual three call outs in five minutes, praise the improvement.

When praise is used appropriately, it can help build a child's self-confidence and security, stimulate initiative, motivate learning and generally make a child feel good. When a child gets positive feedback about his or her efforts and accomplishments, his or her self-concept is enhanced.

Use *descriptive* praise. Descriptive praise is praise that describes to the child his or her efforts, accomplishments, and feelings. By using descriptive praise, you avoid evaluating a student and making judgments about his or her personality (judgmental praise). When you praise a child, deal with real events. Here are some examples that will help you see the difference between descriptive praise and judgmental praise.

Descriptive Praise	*Judgmental Praise*
"Thank you for picking up the trash on the floor."	"You're very neat."
"I like the drawing you made. It looks great."	"You're a good artist."
"I like the way you are practicing your multiplication tables."	"You are a good girl."

When you use descriptive praise, you are telling the child *exactly* what you liked ("I like it when you complete your work") instead of making a judgment about the child's personality ("You're a good boy").

ALWAYS PRAISE THE BEHAVIOR.

Besides praise, there are some nonverbal ways to recognize a good behavior. For example, a pat on the back, a smile of approval, general facial expressions, and others.

Praising a child in a dull monotone voice is not effective. You use a lot of energy and volume when you yell at a kid. Use this same energy in praising a child. Raise your voice, get excited, and make a big deal out of the situation. Occasionally you will find a student who will not respond to public praise. In such cases a quiet word, a wink or a pat on the shoulder, just between you and the child, may be more effective.

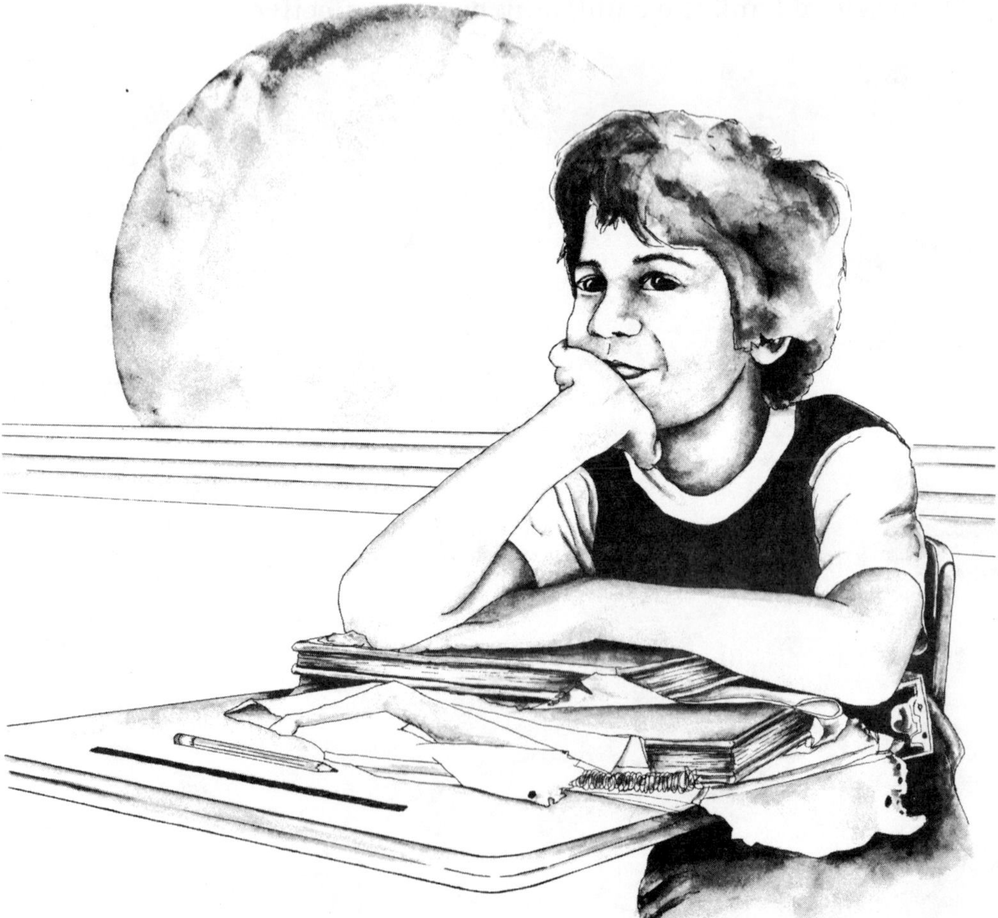

Chapter 4

Improving Behavior and Motivation

How can I Help a Student Improve his or her Behavior and Increase his or her Motivation to do his or her Work?

When some teachers encounter a child who exhibits inappropriate behaviors at school or who is unwilling to do his or her work, they conclude that he or she is a bad child or a lazy child. Such teachers rarely ask themselves "How is my behavior influencing this child?" By asking "how can I help such a student?" you have shown that you are aware that teachers can influence children's behaviors.

Teachers and parents frequently direct excessive attention to a child's undesirable behaviors. A child may be accidentally reinforced for inappropriate behaviors. However, when a desirable behavior occurs, attention may not be given to the child because such behavior is expected. Do you spend too much time attending to bad behaviors and not enough time responding to good behaviors? Take this quiz to find out.

A Ghost Visits Your Classroom

Pretend that a ghost observes you and your class for a day. The ghost has a sheet of paper. Whenever he hears you make a positive comment to a child, he puts a "+" on the sheet.

"Good Jeffrey! As soon as I said it's math time, you took out your math book and got right down to work!"

+	+	+	+	+	+				
+	+	+	+	+	+				
+	+	+	+	+	+				
+	+	+	+	+	+				
+	+	+	+	+					

Whenever he hears you make a negative comment to a child, he puts a "-" on the sheet.

> "What's wrong with you Judy? It always takes you so long to start your work!"

−	−	−	−	−	−	−	−		
−	−	−	−	−	−	−	−	−	
−	−	−	−	−	−	−			
−	−	−	−	−	−	−			
−	−	−	−	−	−	−			

At the end of the day, would you have more +s or more -s? If your -s outnumber your +s, then you may be reinforcing inappropriate behaviors, discouraging appropriate behaviors, and negatively affecting children's feelings of self-worth. You should at least have a balance between the positive and negative comments.

Keeping our +s and -s in mind, let's go over six essential rules to help us find an answer to your question about improving children's behavior and motivation.

The Amazing Half-Dozen Principles

1. Most behaviors are learned.
2. A behavior followed by positive reinforcement is likely to occur again.
3. When teaching a child a new behavior (e.g., raise hand to leave seat), reinforce the specific behavior each time it occurs. Later, reinforce it every few times (e.g., fourth, sixth, third) it occurs.
4. Never take good behavior for granted. Recognize it!
5. Don't pay attention to a behavior you want to weaken (e.g., calling out), ignore it.
6. Punishment many times reinforces a behavior.

If these principles sound new to you or you're not too sure about them, you need to read about behavior management techniques. A good book for this purpose is *Living with Children* by Gerald Patterson (Research Press; Champaign, IL or *Little People* by Edward Christophersen (H & H Enterprises; Inc., Lawrence, KS). It's a good idea to have copies in your classroom to lend to parents who need the information to help them with their children.

Now, let's get down to business. To help a child improve his or her school behavior and motivation, we're going to use a daily progress chart you will check *every* day. For best results, we will need parent involvement. By daily reviewing, signing, and providing appropriate consequences, the parents can be more effective than you can in influencing the child. After all, what power do you really have over a child? You can't take away his or her TV privileges; you can't control the availability of his or her bicycle, etc.

Never just send the chart home with the child! The parents must be trained to review the chart and provide appropriate consequences for the child. Have a conference with the parents. Let the parents know that you're sincerely concerned with the progress of the child.

Explain to the parents how to help back up the school in a planned program. Tell the parents, "It is suggested that your child learn that there are logical consequences for his or her actions. Just because he or she is alive does *not* entitle him or her to privileges (such as TV, playing with friends, going to fun places on the weekend, eating ice cream or dessert, etc.). The child *must* learn that there is a direct connection between his or her behavior and privileges."

"You must know how your child is performing in school on a daily basis. Research tells us that rewards or punishments should occur right after the behavior is exhibited. Rewarding or punishing a child for school performance should be done on a daily basis. In order for you to do this, I will fill out a progress report form to send to you each day." (Several different types of forms can be used depending on your school's schedule and organization.)

Form 1 is best in a school where the child has several teachers a day. The child must present this form to each teacher at the end of each class period. Form 2 is appropriate for grades two and up if the child stays with one teacher for most of the day. Form 3 is appropriate for children in kindergarten or first grade or for more severe problems. On Form 3, you check the child for the *same* behavior(s) several times a day. If you use this form, start with one easy goal the first week and gradually make it more complex (easy goal = keep floor clean; complex goal = complete assignments). Now, let's look at the forms.

DAILY PROGRESS REPORT FORM 1

Student _____ Class or Grade _____

Week Beginning _____

To the teacher: Please check this form each day the child is in your class. Consistency is essential. The student will take this form home daily. During the time the child spent with you or during each subject block, rate the child as follows:

1. In the top half of each box, rate the child's BEHAVIOR.
2. In the bottom half of each box, rate the child's EFFORT in doing classwork. Sign your initials.

Example

Use these two letters only:

S = Satisfactory
U = Unsatisfactory

Behavior → S *RB* ← Teacher's initials
Effort in Classwork → U *RB*

Subject and Teacher	Mon.	Tues.	Wed.	Thurs.	Fri.
Parent's Signature					

DAILY PROGRESS REPORT FORM 2

Student _____ Teacher _____

Week Beginning _____

A check indicates satisfactory performance ✓
A zero indicates unsatisfactory performance 0
NA indicates that the item does not apply today NA

	Mon.	Tues.	Wed.	Thurs.	Fri.
1. Homework turned in					
2. Follows directions					
3. Gets right down to work					
4. Pays attention to teacher					
5. Tries hard to do assignments (effort)					
6. Respects the rights of others					
7. Follows class and school rules					
8. Talks at proper time					
9. Acceptable behavior in special classes (art, music, physical ed., etc.					
10. Other:					
Teacher's initials					

COMMENTS FROM TEACHER   PARENT'S SIGNATURE

Monday _____   _____
Tuesday _____ _____
Wednesday _____   _____
Thursday _____   _____
Friday _____   _____

1. Child takes chart home daily.
2. Parent signs chart daily.
3. Child returns chart to school daily.

DAILY PROGRESS REPORT FORM 3

Child's Name _____ Teacher _____

Week Beginning _____

To the Teacher: If this procedure is not followed and consistency is not maintained, the program will become frustrating for the child and will be bound to fail.

1. At each time indicated, place a "happy face," in ink, if the student met the specified behavioral goal(s). Make a sad face if goals were not met.
2. Please remember that YOU ARE CHECKING THE CHILD ONLY FOR THE BEHAVIORS LISTED BELOW. Any other disruptive behaviors that occur should be treated with your usual disciplinary procedures.
3. As you check this chart during the day, be certain that the student sees you doing it. Verbally state why child is receiving "face." If the student did not follow goal(s), say, "You did not _(state goal)_ ." If the student did follow the goal(s), praise the specific behavior, say, "You (state goal). That's fantastic!"

Time to Check	Mon.	Tues.	Wed.	Thurs.	Fri.
Parent's Signature					

Goal(s):

1. _____
2. _____
3. _____

Here are some additional suggestions for using Form 3.

1. During the first week, present the child with *one* easily achievable goal. The child must experience success and its accompanying feelings if the chart is to become meaningful. At first, goals must be easy to accomplish. Possible easy goals for the first week could include:

   - keep the floor clean
   - stay in line with the class
   - get teacher's permission before leaving the room

   More difficult goals (such as *complete assignments*) should be attempted later on.
2. Understand that new ways of behaving are learned through many successful experiences. Therefore, a child whose major problem is fighting may need to begin with easier goals. After the child has experienced some success with the easier goals, the more difficult goals can be worked on.
3. During the first few weeks, the child's chart should be checked (with a happy or sad face) by you once an hour. As the child becomes successful, the frequency of checking the chart may gradually be reduced (morning and afternoon).
4. Add new goals after the child achieves the present goal(s). Now the child will have to do several things in combination to earn a happy face.

How to Use the Forms

The key to the child's improvement in school is what the parents do when they see the daily progress report. Tell the parents: "First, you must set up a system of pre-planned consequences for your child's behavior. On his or her good days, good things will happen to him or her, and on bad days, bad things will happen. *These consequences should occur daily.* Before the child leaves for school on Monday, he or she *must* be told what consequences to expect on any day this week he or she brings home a good report and on any day this week he or she brings home a bad report."

Remind the parents to tell the child what they consider to be a good and bad day in advance. It is suggested that during the first two weeks of using the progress report, at least 50% of the items on the form should be satisfactory. During the next four weeks, at least 75% of the items on the form should be satisfactory. During subsequent weeks 80% of the items should be satisfactory to consider the day "good."

EXPLAIN TO THE PARENTS THAT "SOME CHILDREN DO POORLY HOPING THAT THEIR PARENTS WILL GIVE UP THIS NEW APPROACH. *DO NOT* LET THE CHILD MANIPULATE YOU. AS THE PARENTS, YOU MUST BE THE BOSSES! IF YOU GIVE UP, YOU ARE TEACHING YOUR CHILD THAT HE OR SHE HAS THE POWER TO CONTROL *YOUR* BEHAVIOR. ONCE YOU MAKE THE RULES, STICK BY THEM."

* * * * *

SOME CHILDREN DO BETTER FOR AWHILE AND SUDDENLY GO BACK TO THEIR OLD BEHAVIORS. THIS IS THE CHILD'S LAST ATTEMPT TO GET THE PARENTS AND THE TEACHER TO GIVE UP THIS APPROACH. CHILDREN WOULD RATHER NOT HAVE CONSEQUENCES TO FACE WHEN THEY MISBEHAVE. *DON'T GIVE UP!* CONTINUE TO USE THE APPROACH EVEN IF IT TAKES SEVERAL WEEKS FOR THE CHILD TO SHOW IMPROVEMENT AGAIN.

The Consequences

It can be very effective for parents to set a child up on an allowance. This allowance can be earned by effort in school. For example, a $2 per week allowance would be equivalent to 40¢ per school day. Each day the child meets his or her goal on the daily report, he or she is given 40¢ towards an allowance. The parents should give the money in daily installments because the child needs an immediate reward. This approach can only be effective if the child *must* use this money for his or her everyday purchases (e.g., ice cream, juice bar at school, comics, pinball machine, snacks, movies, etc.). The parents should never give the child money in advance and *never* give the child extra money because he or she needs to buy something and didn't earn enough this week. For example, if the child wants to go to the movies on Saturday and needs $1.50 but only earned $1.20 this week — too bad! He or she must suffer the consequences of his or her own behavior and miss the movie. The parents may feel guilty by seeing a child feel low, but by suffering the consequences of his or her own behavior, the child will learn some valuable lessons.

How much allowance should a child get? That depends on age and needs. An eleven-year-old child probably needs more spending money than one who is six years old. The parents should figure out how much money the child needs per week for ice cream, comics, amusements, snacks, movies, etc. This amount is probably right for an allowance.

The way the parents respond to their child is also very important. When the child has met his or her goal for the day, the parents should show real enthusiasm and make it seem like the Fourth of July! The parents can respond by saying something like: "Fantastic — you really tried today! Dynamite! You should be very proud of yourself. Today you get your allowance money and all of your other privileges." The parents should encourage the child to try hard again tomorrow.

During the first few weeks of the program, the parents should make a big deal out of their child's achievements. In addition to his or her allowance, when he or she has had a good day, the parents can provide him or her with a special privilege or treat such as:

- pizza
- record
- no chores today
- special dessert
- skating
- going for ice cream
- having a friend sleep over
- staying up later at night
- going out for dinner
- extra TV time
- snack
- small toy
- going to movies
- comic book

If the child continuously fails to meet a daily goal, negative consequences should be applied on these days. It is suggested that when the child doesn't meet his or her goal in school, the parents deny him or her any privileges or pleasures that day. The child should be restricted to the house.

WHEN A CHILD IS RESTRICTED TO THE HOUSE, THERE SHOULD BE *NO* FRIENDS, TELEPHONE, TV, SNACKS OR SODA, STEREO, RADIO, PLAYING GAMES, COLORING, ETC. THERE *SHOULD* BE CHORES (clean the bathroom), HOMEWORK, AND AN EXPLANATION THAT ON THE DAY YOU MISBEHAVE IN SCHOOL, YOU ARE NOT ENTITLED TO ANYTHING YOU ENJOY.

Explain these concepts to the parents.

If this approach does not result in some improvement after five weeks of using it *daily,* ask yourself these questions:

1. Was the report form checked every day?
2. Was the child rated *only* on the goals listed on the chart?
3. When you checked the chart, did you let the child see it each time it was checked?
4. Did you verbally praise the child for his or her successes?
5. When the child got unsatisfactory ratings, did you explain why he or she earned an unsatisfactory rating?
6. Did the child *always* receive the reward or negative consequence he or she was told he or she would receive by the parents?
7. Was physical punishment avoided?
8. Was the child rewarded or punished on a daily basis?

Your answer to all of these questions should be *yes* if you expect this approach to be effective. If you have used the approach properly for at least five weeks and a serious school problem remains, you may need to consult with the school's principal regarding the child's possible need for special services (physical checkup, counseling, tutoring).

> *O.K. You sold me on using progress charts but can I use a similar system to stimulate the whole class too?*

Definitely! You can use *Dynamite Notes. Dynamite Notes* are little tickets with a smile face and the words Dynamite Good Worker!

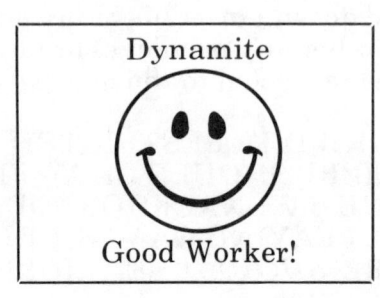

Improving Behavior and Motivation

Here's how to use these notes as part of a systematic behavior improvement program.

1. Pick a daily behavior for your class to work on (e.g., keep your hands and feet to yourself, return materials in usable condition, be quiet in the hall, etc.). The behavior should be specific (e.g., "be good" is *not* specific). Work on the behavior for a few days. When the class masters it, begin to work on a new behavior. In the beginning, work on one behavior at a time. Later on, you can work on several behaviors simultaneously.
2. Make a class chart on a ditto stencil. List the students' names vertically on the left side. Make a column for each hour of the school day. A sample chart follows.

Name	10	11	12	1	2	3
Bobby Jones						
Jeff Reeb						
Howard Gold						
Cathrine Queen						
Gary Barbe						
Catrina Smith						
Michael Turtle						
Lisa Steele						
Barry Bolin						
Susie Shiff						
Ellie Fish						

3. Each morning, announce to the class the behavior to be worked on that day.
4. Whenever a child fails to reach the goal, place a zero next to his or her name on the chart for the appropriate hour. At the end of the hour, those students who did not get a zero should be given a check for meeting the goal that hour.
5. At dismissal time, give a dynamite note to each child who had no more than one zero (during the first two weeks allow children two zeros). Pair the presentation of the dynamite notes with verbal praise to further recognize the child's efforts. Do not place any emphasis on students who failed to meet the goal. Negative behaviors should be ignored as much as possible while positive behaviors are always recognized.

It is suggested that before you start such a program, you send a letter to parents explaining what will be happening (see sample following). They should know that any day their child does not bring home a dynamite note, the child did not meet the day's goal. Encourage parents to praise their child for earning a dynamite note.

Royal Cactus Primary School
Bee Sting, Principal

Dear Parents,

Tomorrow, I will be starting a program with my class to recognize children's efforts. Too often we fail to recognize the good things children do. This program will help avoid this.

Everyday, the class will have a "behavior of the day" to work on. For example, tomorrow, we will work on "keep your hands to yourself." Each child who shows respect for others by keeping his/her hands to him/herself most of the day will be awarded a "dynamite good worker" slip. Each day your child brings home a slip, you'll know that he/she reached the goal of the day.

Please congratulate and praise your child each day he or she earns this award. Let's show the children that their "good" behaviors are appreciated.

Please call me if you have any questions about this program.

Sincerely,

Robin Bird

Robin Bird
Teacher, Class 3-2

You can further spice up this program by having weekly awards. Make up and duplicate a weekly award. Each Friday, present this award to children who earned a *dynamite good worker* slip every day of the week.

Royal Cactus Primary School
Bee Sting, Principal

Thomas Dolinsky
(name)

has earned a Dynamite Good Worker award everyday this week. We congratulate him/her for his/her effort.

6/1/80
date

R. Bird
R. Bird, Teacher

I'm a busy classroom teacher. I don't have the time for such a program.

That's a poor excuse. Teachers who run this program find that it saves them time! As your class behavior improves, you'll save time reminding and correcting children. By sending home good news, you'll improve parents' feelings about the school and about you. This will make it easier for you to get parents involved in the school program and to approach them when something bad happens. Most of all, you'll be glad that you're not a negative teacher — you'll be responding to the good things kids do!

Chapter 5

Conflict Avoidance

How can I Teach Children Alternatives to Violence for Solving Conflicts?

Children already have and use a multitude of peaceful techniques for dealing with conflict. Adults generally don't pay attention to this. However, the one time a child uses physical force as a solution, adult attention is secured. We should give children attention when we see them avoiding physical conflicts so they can learn that conflict avoidance is something good. Schools that implement programs and place an emphasis on children who solve conflicts in nonviolent manners significantly reduce the number of fights that occur by teaching children that they have alternatives to violence.

School-Wide Emphasis on Solving Conflicts

We must recognize children for solving conflicts without violence. When a child accomplishes this, we'll call the child a *Conflict Resolver*. The principal should distribute conflict resolver forms to each teacher.

```
To:       The Office
From:     Teacher's Name
Date:

____Student's name_____ resolved a conflict today.

This is what happened. _____
_____
_____

Please announce his/her name on the public address system
and present him/her with a Conflict Resolver Certificate.
```

Conflict Resolver Certificate

_____

resolved a conflict today without fighting or using violence.
We are very proud of this student.

_____   _____
Teacher   Principal

_____
Date

Whenever a teacher catches a child resolving a conflict (without violence), the teacher sends a note to the office and briefly states how the child resolved the conflict (e.g., "When another child called Danny a name, Danny ignored him"). The principal should read the note on the public address system when regular announcements are made. By emphasizing the technique the child used to resolve the conflict, other children will be exposed to alternatives for dealing with conflict. The child should be presented with a certificate or note to the parents explaining the child's accomplishment. This usually encourages the child's family to reinforce the child's efforts.

Classroom Emphasis on Resolving Conflicts

When you see a child avoid a fight or solve a conflict in a peaceful manner, recognize it. Say something to the child about his or her positive behavior. You can also use charting techniques to encourage children to use non-violent techniques in dealing with conflicts. This technique will involve using two charts, a *conflict resolver's* chart and a *how to resolve a conflict* chart.

Discuss the meaning of the word *conflict* with your class. After defining the word, have the class generate a list of ways to resolve conflicts. Make this list into a large chart (*How to Resolve a Conflict*) which can be displayed in the classroom. To help the children come up with ways to resolve conflicts, give them some problems to solve.

1. One kid tells another that, "your mother looks like an ape." Why would someone call you a name? What can you do? Explain to your kids that "someone calls you a name to get you angry and upset. If the kid who's calling you a name sees you get angry, he or she'll feel happy. But how would he or she feel if you didn't get angry? Right, then he or she would be angry because he or she couldn't upset you."
    These are some techniques for resolving conflicts related to example 1.
    a. Ignore. Don't pay any attention to the other kid. Don't even look at him or her; just walk away.
    b. Make a joke. Make a joke about yourself or agree with whatever the name caller says. Don't call him or her back a name.
      "You're right, not only does my mother look like an ape, she also smells like an ape." (joke)
      "You're right, she looks like an ape." (agree)
2. Someone pushes ahead of you on the line at the water fountain. What can you do?
    a. Ignore (let the other kid go).
    b. Flip a coin (to see who goes first).
    c. Explain (tell the other child you were there first and ask him or her to get behind you).
3. Someone starts a fight with you.
    a. Discuss (talk about the problem and see if you can solve it without fighting).
    b. Get help. Get someone else (an adult) to help you with the problem.

c. Delay (put the fight off until later and you'll probably have calmed down and won't need to fight).
d. Ignore (walk away and don't fight).
e. Give and take (each person gives up something in order to resolve the problem).

The sample conflict resolution techniques enumerated above are a few ideas, but your students will think of many original ways to resolve conflicts. The techniques will be listed and numbered on the *How to Resolve a Conflict* chart. For example, using just the strategies listed here, a chart would contain the following:

How to Resolve a Conflict

1. Ignore
2. Make a Joke about Yourself
3. Flip a Coin
4. Explain
5. Discuss
6. Get Help
7. Delay
8. Give and Take

It is important to number the techniques.

Now, you're ready to make a *Conflict Resolver's Chart*. This chart names children who resolve conflicts. Make a graph chart. List the names of all the children in the class down the left side of the chart. Whenever you spot a child resolving a conflict by one of the techniques on the *How to Resolve a Conflict Chart,* have him or her put the number of the technique used next to his name. So, if Tom made a joke about himself, he'd put number two next to his name. Whenever a child puts a number next to his or her name, he or she should be given a *Conflict Resolver's Award* (certificate, pin, happygram, or whatever you can make up.)

You'll probably come across a child who says, "My father said I should fight if someone starts up with me." "Fine," you reply, but "at school, I'm in charge. You'll have to follow my rules at school." Even if a child never uses the better techniques, you've exposed that child to alternatives to violence. Without your efforts, some children may never be aware of the wide range of alternatives to violence.

Chapter 6

Improving School Attendance

How can I help improve children's attendance at school?

For many children, school is a dull and boring place. For others, it may be a negative environment where failure is often experienced and success is rarely experienced. Some children prefer to escape the school environment and become truant. Other children and their parents may not take school attendance seriously. Obviously, the first step you must take to improve children's attendance is to make your classroom and your school a stimulating, positive, caring, and friendly place. Next, you might implement specific programs and strategies to motivate children to come to school. We will look at procedures that can be used for an entire school, including students with chronic absenteeism.

School-Wide Program

A school-wide attendance motivation program helps make students and parents more aware of the importance of school attendance in general and of their own attendance in particular. It is unfortunate that many schools offer students awards for perfect attendance while neglecting to recognize improved attendance. If this is happening at your school, change that approach! Try this program for your school.

1. Distribute to parents a written statement of your school's attendance policy (e.g., student must submit note from parent explaining absence).

2. On the first day the student is absent, telephone the home. This call can be made by the teacher, secretary, volunteer, etc. The purpose of the call is to determine the reason for a child's absence. If it is discovered that a child stayed home for a medical or dental appointment, encourage the child to return to school at the conclusion of that appointment (even if it's the last hour of the school day when the child returns, encourage that return). *It must be emphasized that the call to the child's home should be made the first day of the absence.* Repeat the call at least every other day to check on the child's status.
3. Set up a 100% attendance photo bulletin board in a place that every child will pass (e.g., cafeteria). Every two months, take pictures of children who achieved 100% attendance during that time period. To minimize the cost, take the photos outdoors so flashbulbs will not be necessary, use black and white film, and have three children stand together for a snapshot. Change the photos every two months. This photo bulletin board is an excellent way to recognize children for something good.
4. *Everyday,* announce the classes having 100% attendance on the school's public address system. Then, send these classes a "100% Attendance" banner to display. They should return the banner at the end of the day.
5. When report cards are issued, present certificates for the marking period to students who achieve 100% attendance.
6. Students who show improved attendance during a marking period should be awarded a certificate. Improved attendance may be defined as having half the number of absences of the previous marking period.
7. At regular intervals (e.g., once every two weeks) recognize the classes (e.g., best class on each grade level) with the best attendance during that time period. The recognition could be:

- ice cream party
- movie film
- puppet show
- athletic event or game
- group sing
- guest speaker

O.K. But what do I do about the child who is a chronic absentee?

This child needs more than the school-wide program discussed above. But before you decide that a child has a real attendance problem, determine why the child is absent so much. If there's an illness involved, then perhaps the child really needs to stay home a lot. If there's a family problem, a referral for family counseling might be appropriate. If it's really a poor attendance pattern, then some special strategies might help. Here are some things you can do.

1. Have an individual conference with the child. Explain that you would like to help him or her improve his or her attendance. Let the child tell you about his or her feelings regarding his or her attendance and if he or she wishes to improve it.
2. Contact the child's parents. Parent support and participation is needed for you to be successful. Invite the parents to school for a conference. If the parents cannot come, explain your program on the telephone or make a home visit.
3. Work out a behavioral contract with the child. The contract should consist of an attendance goal during a specified time interval and a reward for meeting that goal.

Sample Contract

I _____(name)_____ agree to the following:

a. I will come to school every day. If I miss school it will be because I was sick or had a doctor's appointment. I will bring a note from my parents or doctor to explain why I was absent.
b. Each morning, I will put a check next to my name on the attendance chart (see explanation below).
c. Every week I have perfect attendance, I will get a *Perfect Week of Attendance Certificate* and I will be allowed to help the physical education teacher for 30 minutes.
d. Whenever I have two weeks of perfect attendance, I will get a prize in addition to the certificate and helper time.
e. Whenever I have two weeks of perfect attendance, my teacher will call my parents to tell them how my attendance has been improving.

I understand that this is a binding contract between _____(teacher)_____ and myself and I agree to the rules.

_____ _____
Student   Teacher

As indicated in item b of the contract, you will post an *Attendance Improver's Chart.* By having the child check his or her own attendance daily, he or she can easily follow progress and be self-reinforced. The teacher must consistently follow the terms of the contract.
4. Try to make school more meaningful to the child. Arrange for the child to have responsibilities. These should be responsibilities that give the child status with the class.

Sample Responsibilities

- patrol monitor
- pet keeper
- office helper (15 minutes daily)
- principal's helper (15 minutes daily)

Such jobs can help create a desire to attend school.

5. Arrange for the child to have a buddy. This peer might:
   - walk to school with the child
   - call the child on the telephone regularly
   - work on a class project with the child
   - tutor the child
6. If the child should be absent, be sure to call him or her. Show your sincere concern for the absence and let him or her know that he or she was missed.
7. Verbally praise the child's attendance. "Wow! Today's Wednesday. Only two more days and you'll have another perfect week of attendance! You should be very proud of yourself. I'm so pleased that you are coming to school every day. Keep up the good work!" Recognize the child's efforts. Show him or her that you are really excited about improvements.
8. Create some competition. When two or more children are working on this program, the competitive atmosphere often serves as an additional motivator. Also, encourage the child to compete with himself or herself. "You've been in school every day for three weeks. If you keep it up through next week, you'll have a perfect month of attendance."

You're probably thinking about all the extra work involved. But what's your alternative? If you don't intervene, the child may never have the opportunity to improve. The chronic absentee needs your help to break the being absent habit.

Sample Certificates

Use the duplicating machine at your school to create certificates.

IMPROVED ATTENDANCE

_____

has improved his/her attendance this grading period.

_____ _____
Teacher   Principal

100% ATTENDANCE

_____

has had 100% attendance this grading period.

_____ _____
Teacher   Principal

PERFECT WEEK

_____

has attended school every day this week. We are all very proud of him/her.

CONGRATULATIONS!

_____
Date

_____ _____
Teacher   Principal

When the child has shown an improvement for three months, you can reduce your efforts. You can revise the contract and arrange for a monthly goal and monthly reward. Let the child retain his job all year. Rotate jobs occasionally to avoid boredom.

One more thing. You're a good teacher! Take pride! By implementing programs such as this, you show that you really care. You do more than complain or just discuss a problem, you take action, you intervene. Give yourself a star!

Chapter 7

Lying and Tattling

How can I Help Reduce Children's Lying and Tattling?

Children are often taught to lie. Who teaches children to lie? Some parents and teachers do without realizing it! For example, a child may be punished for telling the truth. The child might conclude that if he lies, he may avoid punishment. This happened to Kevin. One day Kevin broke his teacher's fan by knocking it off a desk while chasing another kid. When the teacher, Mr. Big, returned to the classroom, Kevin told him what happened. Mr. Big responded, "How dare you run around the room! Just for that you are going to sit at a table by yourself for the rest of the year and you cannot be a safety patrol monitor any more!" Kevin was punished for telling the truth. His honesty was never recognized and the consequences were not related to the act. Mr. Big could have responded in a more appropriate manner by saying: "Kevin, I appreciate your honesty in telling me what happened. You should be proud that you can face up to your mistake. Of course, you are responsible for damaging my electric fan. The fan costs $15 and I expect you to pay for it. I will speak with your parents and suggest that you work to earn the money by doing extra chores. I don't want your parents to just give you the money."

Some children lie because they get attention for lying. When a child is obviously lying or exaggerating, the adult should listen passively but not respond with a verbal remark or facial expression. Don't allow the child's lying to get him attention from others.

A child who frequently lies and exaggerates may feel unimportant. As the teacher, you can help this child learn to feel important. Praise the child for efforts and accomplishments. Notice special things (e.g., "That's a nice shirt you're wearing"). Give the child special jobs to do. When you meet with the child's parents, share your observations about the child's problem. If the parents are open to suggestions, talk to them about ways to make the child feel important. The parents can accomplish this if they:

1. Listen to the child when he speaks.
2. Praise good behaviors and achievements.
3. Spend some private time with the child. During this time there should be interaction. Go for a walk, go bike riding, play tennis, play chess.
4. Give the child responsibilities. Show him that he or she is a capable person.

Your school should pay attention to honesty. For example, Debbie finds a quarter on the floor and gives it to the teacher. The teacher should praise Debbie and give Debbie a note for her parents describing her action. When something more substantial occurs (e.g., a child finds a watch and turns it into the school's office), it is worthy of school-wide attention. The principal may announce the child's action on the public address system and present the child with a certificate or letter of recognition.

Tattling is a behavior that adults often encourage because they listen to the child. A teacher should consistently refuse to listen to what one child says about another child. So, if Billy approaches Ms. Fair's desk and says, "Ms. Fair, Becky put a crayon in her pocket," Ms. Fair should respond, "I'm not interested in hearing about that." Ms. Fair shouldn't pursue this charge any further because it would reward Billy for tattling.

Remember, if the child gets satisfaction by exhibiting any behavior, he or she will probably continue that behavior. Don't let a child get satisfaction for inappropriate behaviors.

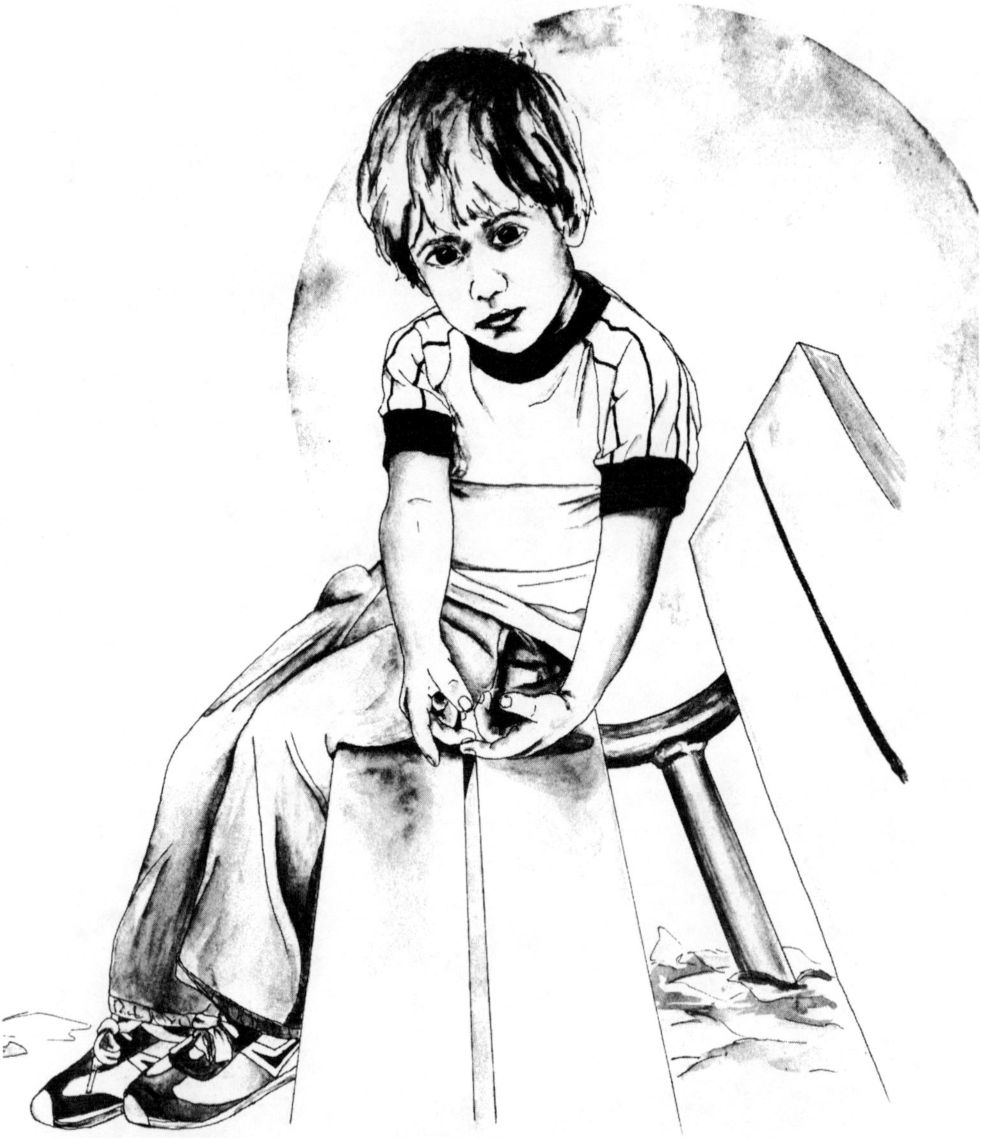

Chapter 8

School Phobia

What can I do to Help a Child who is Afraid to Come to School?

The school-phobic child is probably being rewarded for not coming to school. The child may find school an uncomfortable place to be. This could be because of failure, dislike of the teacher, poor peer relationships or a multitude of other reasons. When the child is allowed to stay home from school, he or she is allowed to escape an environment that he or she does not prefer. Some children find the home more attractive than the school. If a child is allowed pleasures (e.g., television, snacks, games, during the day) when at home, the home may be more attractive than the school environment. When this occurs, staying home from school is actually rewarded.

There are some children whose school phobia is so severe that the suggestions made in this chapter will not meet their needs. The longer a child has been a school phobic, the more difficult it is to eliminate the problem. In a severe case, the child needs to be referred to a psychologist or mental health worker who can help structure a behavioral program that may require additional support and shaping.

Reducing School Phobia

The child must be gradually introduced to the school environment. During the first three days of this program, the parents should walk around the school with the child but not enter. On the fourth and fifth days, they should enter the school, walk around the building for a few minutes, and leave.

During the weekend, they should walk around the school to maintain contact. (The time frame suggested here may have to be changed based on a child's progress or lack of progress).

On the sixth day, the child should be a helper in the school's office for 30 minutes and go home. On the seventh day, he or she should go to his or her class for 30 minutes and help in the office for 30 minutes. By this time, the parents should leave the child alone while the child is in the school building. Each day, increase the child's stay in school by one hour. So, on the eighth day, he or she'll be in class for 1½ hours and help in the office for 30 minutes. On the tenth day, he or she'll be in class for 3½ hours and help in the office for 30 minutes. Continue this until the child reaches the goal of staying in school all day. Some schools may feel that the child either comes to school for the day or stays home. This is not a helping attitude. The school-phobic child must be gradually desensitized to school.

The teacher must make the child's time in the classroom during this phasing-in period positive. Praise the child's good behaviors (e.g., starting work, behaving appropriately, following directions, etc.). Give the child some classroom responsibilities (e.g., board monitor, caring for class pet, etc.). Avoid giving the child assignments beyond his or her academic level. Until the child feels good about coming to school, you should give assignments that the child can handle without frustration.

Unless the parents handle the school phobic appropriately, the school's efforts will have little, if any, value. It is the school's role to counsel the parents. Never assume that the parents have methods for dealing with problems. Emphasize to the parents that on days the child stays home from school, there should be no TV, stereo, telephone, radio, bicycle, games, going out to play, snacks, or other pleasant things. The child's stay in the house should be uncomfortable. Even after school hours, the child must remain restricted to the house. The child should essentially be in time out for the entire day and night of the day he or she did not go to school. During the phasing-in period, the child should be allowed to have all of his or her privileges if he or she stays in school for the specified amount of time that day.

The daily progress chart, described in Chapter 4, can be helpful. Once the child is attending school regularly, rewarding his or her behavior and work habits is important.

Help the child make friends, if he or she has a problem in this area. Teaming him or her up with a popular child for a project or assignment is a good start. Peer tutoring can be helpful. The school-phobic child can tutor younger children in another class to build up a sense of belonging to the school. Also, an advanced student can tutor the "phobic" student who needs help in a subject area.

You *can* help the child who is afraid to come to school. It takes extra time and effort but it is worth it because the job is all about caring about kids and helping them develop positive attitudes toward school so they learn all they are capable of learning.

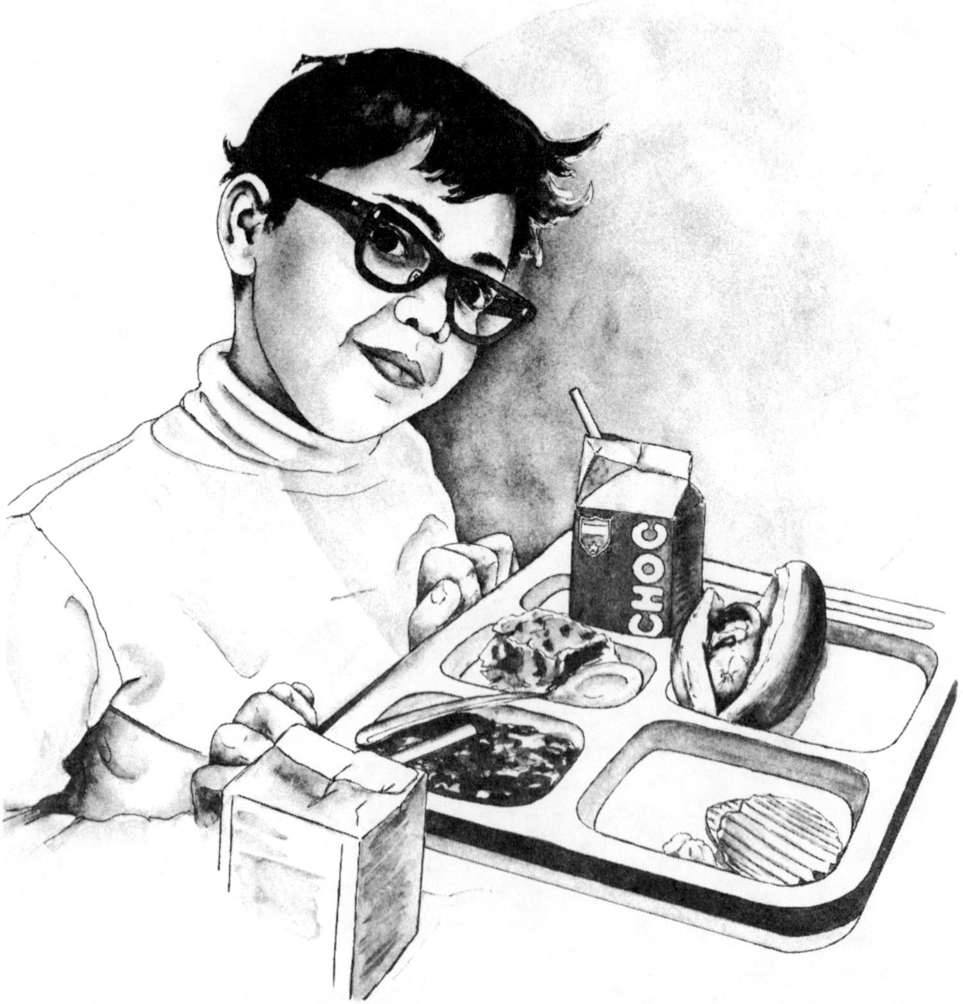
CHOC

Chapter 9

Improving Cafeteria Behavior

How can I help Children Improve their Behavior in the School Cafeteria?

Here is how to set up a cafeteria behavior improvement program:

1. Make a traffic light with red, yellow, and green bulbs. If this is not practical, use large flags (red, yellow, and green).
   - Red = Silence
   - Yellow = Talk softly only to the person next to you or opposite you
   - Green = No restrictions on talking
2. Print up score sheets (1 sheet per class per day).

Class Score Sheet   date _____

- Enter cafeteria quietly and orderly.   _____
- Keep floors clean.   _____
- Obey traffic light during first half of period. _____
- Obey traffic light during second half of period. _____
- Clean tables properly.   _____
- Leave in an orderly manner.   _____

One point per satisfactory item.
Today's total is   _____

Monitor's Score Sheet

Number of positive comments or gestures given   _____

Number of reprimands, warnings given   _____

Score (positives minus negatives)   _____

The cafeteria aide or teacher will score each class individually on a daily basis. When a class enters the cafeteria, the aide should give the class a score sheet. When a class breaks one of the rules on the score sheet, the aide should immediately put a zero next to the appropriate item. At the end of the lunch period, the aide should put a "1" next to the rules the class adhered to and enter the total points the class earned for the day.

This is meant to be a positive program. The aide should be instructed to catch kids and classes doing good things in the cafeteria. Instead of hearing the aide constantly yelling and screaming, a visitor to the cafeteria should hear things like:

"Wow! Bobby, when you finished your lunch you took out a book to read. You sure make good use of your time!"

"Susie! Someone threw food at you and you ignored it. That's fantastic!"

"Danny, someone talked to you when the red light was on and you ignored him. Dynamite!"

To have a successful cafeteria program, look for good behaviors and recognize them. If you use the score sheet without really concentrating on recognizing appropriate behaviors, the program's effectiveness will be minimal. In order to provide self-feedback the monitor should tally each time he or she gives positive or negative comments and/or feedback to any member of a class. The number of negative contacts should be subtracted from the positive contact tally to provide a score. The higher the score the more certain it is the monitor is maintaining good lunchroom behavior.

3. Reward the top scoring classes of the week. For example, select the class on each grade level that earned the most points during the week. Let each student in these classes wear a badge. Badges can be made of laminated construction paper and a pin can be used to attach the badge to clothing. Imprinted on the badge should be words of

distinction such as *Cafeteria Behavior Champion*. Also, give each of these classes a weekly award certificate to hang in their classroom.

Oak Garden School
Mrs. Pine Tree, Principal

Cafeteria Behavior
Award

Presented to

_____
(class)

For having the most points in the cafeteria during the week of _____.

Mrs. Pine Tree
Principal

Every Friday afternoon, read each class, weekly point total on the public address system.

As with any school program, teacher support and enthusiasm is needed. Teachers should strongly encourage their classes to earn many points. A competitive spirit, similar to that of a football game, is essential. Teachers should review, with their students, the daily score sheet. Children should be encouraged to ignore others who try to distract them and get them to break a cafeteria rule. Ask your kids to put one finger up when the red light comes on. This is helpful since some children at a table may not see the light. The finger might attract their attention.

If we can't run a complete program, what are some other things my school can do to make the cafeteria a better place?

Try some films. You can show films that would be of interest to children during the lunch hour. Play the film's sound softly.

When the cafeteria noise level rises above the film's sound, stop the film until it is quiet enough to continue.

You can also try using fines. Give every class 500 points. Have a master chart listing each class point total. Then print up some fines.

Cafeteria Fine

Name _____

You have broken one of our cafeteria rules.

_____ Running
_____ Talking during silent period
_____ Dirty table or floor area
_____ Throwing things
_____ Other:

Your class is fined one point for each rule you broke.

When a child breaks an established cafeteria rule, he or she is given a fine by an aide or teacher. The child must give the fine to his or her teacher. The adult issuing the fine subtracts one point per violation from the master chart. On a weekly basis, announce the total points retained by each class. At the end of four weeks, reward the two top classes with an ice cream party or other special treat or privilege. Then, give each class 500 points and start all over again. If you don't start over, some classes will be so far behind that they'll give up. By renewing the program, everyone has hope.

Spot awards can also be very effective. Make up some *Good Cafeteria Behavior Certificates*. When you catch a child doing something good, give that child a cafeteria award on the spot.

Examples of good things you should catch kids doing in the cafeteria.
- ignoring someone who is bothersome
- picking trash up from the floor
- reading after eating
- finishing the entire lunch
- covering mouth to cough or sneeze

Here's a great idea! Make a ten-minute tape recording about the rules in the cafeteria. Interview, on tape, the cafeteria aide, a server on the food line, the custodian, and the principal.

Have each of these people tell how he or she expects children to behave in the cafeteria. Then, interview a child whose behavior in the cafeteria is excellent. Have this child tell how he or she behaves in the cafeteria and what he or she would do if another child threw food at him or her, talked to him or her during a silent period, and pushed in front of him or her on the serving line.

After you make the tape, prepare several written questions about the tape. Now, when a child is misbehaving in the cafeteria, send him or her to an isolated area to listen to the tape and answer the written questions. This is a constructive approach because you have given the child an opportunity to learn the rules and to study them. Next time he or she misbehaves, you can use other disciplinary procedures (e.g., exclusion from the cafeteria for a day). But at least you will have taken a professional approach by trying to *teach,* not just punish.

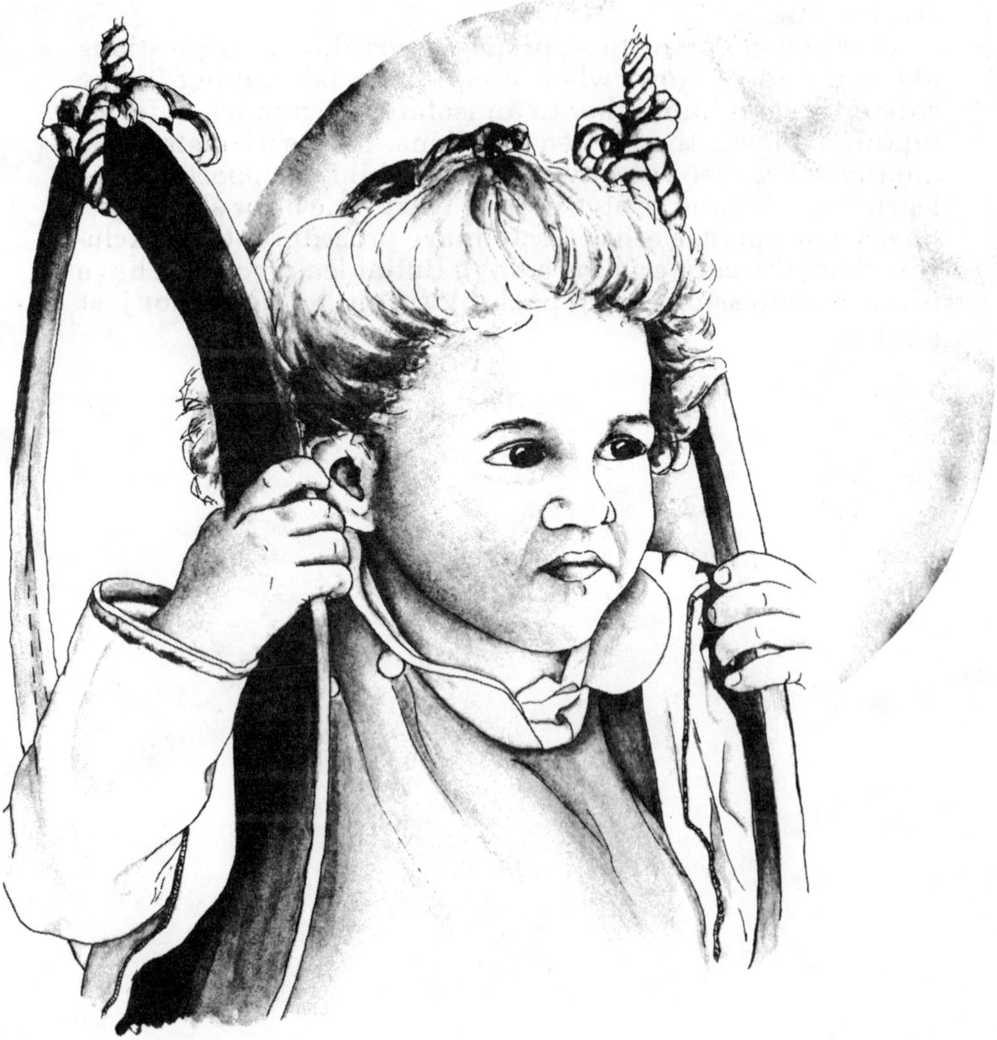

Chapter 10

Shy and Non-assertive Children

How can I Help the Shy and Non-assertive Child?

All teachers should be concerned with shy and non-assertive children, but many teachers focus their concerns on acting-out behaviors and find little time to deal with the child who is living in a shell. This child needs as much attention as the acting-out child.

Friend of the Day

If the child needs to make more friends, the *Friend of the Day Game* may help. At the end of each day, ask the child to select the one child in the class who acted the friendliest to him or her all day. Present this friend with a certificate or happy-gram for being a good friend. The shy child must select a different friend each day.

Target Behaviors

What does your shy child need to do more often to be more outgoing and accepted by other children? The answer to this question depends on the individual child's needs. Some behaviors that may lead to better social adjustment include:
- Talking to other children
- Participating in activities with others
- Standing up for rights
- Smiling
- Good eye contact when talking to someone
- Answering questions in class

Of course, this list could go on and on. What you need to do is to identify *one* specific behavior that the child needs to do more frequently. Then, reward (praise, happy-gram, special privilege, etc.) that behavior. At first, reward it every few times it occurs. When the behavior is well established, reward it several times a week and begin to work on rewarding another behavior. The case of Barry will illustrate this technique for you.

Poor Barry

Barry never participated in group activities and was very shy. His teacher, Miss Friendly, decided to help him adjust better to social situations. She decided that the first thing to work on was to increase the frequency that Barry talked to other children. During the first week of this task, Miss Friendly rewarded Barry each time she saw him speak to another child. Sometimes, she praised him ("Barry, you were speaking to Douglas. I'm glad to see you being so friendly"). Other times, she provided an activity reward. ("Barry, since you were friendly and talked to Joanne, you can pass these papers out to the class"). Sometimes she wrote a happy-gram to Barry's parents. ("Today, Barry spoke to a lot of children. I'm glad to see him acting friendly"). By the second week, Barry was doing a lot of talking. Now, Miss Friendly rewarded Barry every few times he talked. Sometimes, she rewarded him every fifth time she saw him talking. On other days she rewarded him every tenth time. Barry never knew when the reward would come. He kept on talking.

Now that Barry was doing a lot of talking, Miss Friendly was ready to work on Barry's participation in group activities. She arranged social studies committees for a project. Barry was assigned to a committee with four other children. Miss Friendly used the same approach she used to get Barry to talk more. Whenever Barry said something to the group or contributed to the group, she rewarded him. Miss Friendly also worked on getting Barry to participate in group games. She arranged for Barry to become a member of the school safety patrol. Barry enjoyed this special assignment.

Increasing Assertiveness

Some children cannot stand up for their own rights and they allow others to abuse them. Many school counselors run assertiveness training groups for such children. Role playing is often used as a technique for teaching a child to be more assertive. Situations are acted out and the focus child must think of effective ways to handle the situation presented. Other children can help by offering suggestions for how the child can deal with the problem. The child who needs to learn to be assertive is the focus child. Sample situations follow.

1. You're on the playground and a kid in your class grabs your basketball and runs away.
2. Your teacher writes your name down for talking but it wasn't you who talked, it was a kid who sat near you.
3. Another kid cuts in front of you on the lunch line.
4. Your friend insists that you play chess but you hate chess; you want to play checkers.
5. You're working on a report in the library. The two kids at the next table are making a lot of noise.

The child who usually withdraws when he or she should be assertive may need a little encouragement. When you see him or her speak up for himself or herself or act assertively, call him or her over to the side and give positive feedback. (e.g., "Marlene, when Marcia threw a spitball at you, you spoke up and told her that it makes you feel annoyed and you expect her to stop it. I'm glad to see you handle your problems by yourself").

Two other chapters in this manual can help you help the shy and non-assertive child. Chapter 5 deals with teaching children alternatives to violence for solving conflicts. Chapter 8 deals with how to help children who are afraid to come to school. Although the shy child is usually not given attention because he or she's not disturbing the class, he or she needs your help as much as any behavior problem child. You *can* help.

One other suggestion: Be sure to avoid calling the withdrawing child, "shy". It is quite probable that one reason some children withdraw is that they have been labeled "shy." Once that happens they will very likely begin living up to the label.

Chapter 11

Manners and Respect for Others

How can I Teach Children Good Manners and Respect for Others?

You're off to a good start by recognizing that good manners and respect for others can be taught. Modeling is very important. Children should see adults demonstrating good manners and respect for others. You must respond to your students with respect. A teacher who says "Where did you leave your brains today, in the garbage can?" to ridicule a child is not demonstrating respect for another person's dignity. You must remember to say "please" and "thank you." Although behaviors modeled by a child's parents are stronger influences than your behavior, your modeling good behaviors will have an effect on the child.

Classroom Manners Game

A little competition and teacher enthusiasm can stimulate children to make a special effort to demonstrate good manners.

1. Divide your class into teams (do it by seating area or any convenient way). A class of 30 students might have four teams.
2. Discuss with your class "What are Manners?" On a large sheet of oak tag use a magic marker to list specific manners cited by the children. Let them come up with the items for the list. Number each item. Here's a sample list from a fourth grade class:
   a. Wash hands after using the bathroom.
   b. Say "please" when you want something.

      c. Say "thank you" when someone is nice to you.
      d. Pick up something if someone drops it.
      e. Hold the door open for the person behind you.
      f. Push in your chair when you leave your seat.
      g. Be friendly to a new child in the class.
      h. When someone talks to you, look at that person.
3. Make a score card for each team and post the cards in a conspicuous place. Whenever you catch a child displaying one of the manners on the list, give the team one point. Carry a pad and pencil when you travel through the school building with your class. This will enable you to write down the names of children who display good manners and when you return to the classroom you can record the points for the appropriate teams. You will have to keep your eyes open for good manners and spend a little extra time to keep score. It's worth it. Your class will be aware of their behavior and you will, through the team approach, be stimulating peer pressure for good manners.
4. The Reward. The team with the most points at the end of the day should be awarded good manners certificates. A daily award is the most effective way to handle this program. If you waited until the end of the week to select the week's champ, the program's effectiveness would be reduced. Once one team is significantly ahead of the others, the other teams feel that it's hopeless and that they'll never catch up. This discouragement could lead to aggressiveness or unmannerly behavior to show that "I don't care." By renewing the contest on a daily basis, every team has a chance.

You can make the awards (certificates) on a ditto or duplicating machine. The kids will be proud of being champs. A fancy award is not necessary. As a long-term goal, you might say that "the team which was champ the greatest number of days this month will get an ice cream party (or a special prize, activity, etc.).

School-Wide Program

A school-wide program to recognize children who show respect and caring for others should be an ongoing program all year. Educators must emphasize and recognize such behavior. Unfortunately, such behavior is often taken for granted and bad behavior gets attention.

CAO (Caring About Others)

CAO is a school-wide program to help recognize children who have demonstrated that they care about others. Here's how your school can implement it.

1. Build up enthusiasm for the program by using a mystery approach. Don't tell the teachers or students about the program for now. Put up signs all around the school. Here are some suggestions for the signs:
   a. CAO CAO CAO
   b. CAO IS COMING
   c. WATCH OUT FOR CAO
   d. CAO IS "SOMETHING ELSE"
   e. BE-A-CAO-BE-A-CAO-CAO-CAO

   Make announcements on the public address system (CAO is coming, Be-a-CAO). Keep the mystery up for three days and then reveal the program to the school.

2. Hold a faculty meeting and discuss CAO (the procedures are explained below). Emphasize that such a program cannot work without teacher enthusiasm and participation. The teachers must get excited about the program. This excitement will transfer to the children.

3. Teachers, students, and staff members can nominate children, faculty, and anyone associated with the school for a CAO award. A CAO award is in recognition of someone doing something nice for another person without being asked to. Examples of such deeds are:
   a. A parent's car gets a flat tire and the principal changes the tire.
   b. A new student joins the class and Ronald stays with him or her for the day, shows him or her the school, and helps him or her get organized.
   c. A child finds a ring and brings it to the office.

4. The names of CAO award recipients are announced on the public address system. The recipients should report to the office. They should be given a button to wear for the day.

At the end of the school day, the button is returned to the office. The buttons can be made out of construction paper, or by a professional badge maker, or other ways. When the child returns the button to the office, he or she is given a certificate to take home.

ELM STREET ELEMENTARY SCHOOL

Caring
About
Others

AWARD for

_____

This child demonstrated that he/she cares about others. Please praise your child for having demonstrated this characteristic.

_____   _____
         date   Principal

Keep a camera in the office and take a picture of award recipients. Post these pictures on a CAO bulletin board.

It's too bad that many adults do not emphasize children's positive behaviors. When adults start looking for positive behaviors, they *can* do it. They can spot positive behaviors and recognize them. This is the only way to encourage good kids to want to continue being good.

Chapter 12

Hyperactive Children

What can I do to Help a Hyperactive Child Adjust to a Regular Class?

For the purposes of this manual, a hyperactive child is a child who has been diagnosed as hyperactive by a physician. Many children who are very hyper are not necessarily hyperactive. Since it's beyond the scope of this manual to discuss clinical aspects of hyperactivity, it is suggested that you do some additional reading to learn more about this syndrome. Some of the activities suggested in this chapter may be beneficial for a child who has been clinically diagnosed as hyperactive.

Helping the Medicated Child

Many hyperactive children are on prescribed medication. Parents should let you know that their child is taking medication because your feedback can be valuable to the physician. Frequently, the child's dose has to be adjusted. You can help by observing:

1. Responsiveness to rewards and punishments
2. Social relationships (extrovert or introvert)
3. Academic performance
4. Level of aggression
5. Appetite for food
6. Physical complaints or abnormalities
   a. stomach-aches
   b. headaches
   c. tremor of fingers

    d. nervous habits (e.g., nail-biting, eyelid twitch or blink, etc.)
    e. skin tone (pale)
    f. significant weight change

If the child forgets to take the medicine, don't allow him or her to use this as an excuse. Hyperactive children have been known to say, "I can't help what I did, I'm hyperactive."

The Child's Need for Movement

Many hyperactive children need to have a lot of movement. Unlike non-hyperactive kids, the hyperactive child cannot (at least initially) be expected to sit in his or her seat for a whole hour. Therefore, you must readjust your curriculum and schedule for the child. If you don't, *you* may make matters worse rather than better. If it is physiologically impossible for a child to sit still for long periods, he or she will act out and become a behavior problem if forced to sit still.

Divide the child's assignments into units of 10 or 15 minutes. You can increase or decrease the time according to what the child demonstrates he or she can handle. So, if the rest of the class is working on 50 math problems, the hyperactive child might work on ten problems, take a break, come back and work on ten more. A break can consist of activities involving movement such as going around the room to pick up trash, taking a message to the office, working on a model or puzzle, etc. The hyperactive child may learn more by doing less work. If he or she's forced to sit for one hour to do 50 math problems, the frustration might interfere with the quality of the work and result in behavior that is disruptive to the whole class. Thus, the child can accomplish more with shorter assignments done with a higher level of attention.

The hyperactive child should have more physical education time than other children. Perhaps he or she can be included in physical education with other classes. The extra physical education periods can also be used as a reward. "If you get 15 math examples correct, then you can have an extra period of physical education today." If physical education classes are not available at your school, the child can go to recess with another class in addition to his or her own class recess.

Progress Charts

The daily progress charts referred to in Chapter 4 can be

very helpful with the hyperactive child. Use the chart according to the instructions in the chapter but be sure to give the child goals he or she is capable of accomplishing.

The Kitchen Timer

A kitchen timer is a valuable aid in behavior modification programs with hyperactive children.

Sample Goal: Stay on task (do your work).

Procedure: Explain the goal and tell the child that you'll be watching to see if he or she stays on task. Whenever he or she hears the bell of the timer ring, he or she should look at you for a signal. If you nod your head "yes," it means he or she has been on task since you started the timer. Whether on task or not, the child regularly gets a five-minute break.

The break should be an activity. Set up an activity table. The table should have puzzles, drawing materials, model building, popular music records that can be listened to with an earphone, clay, individual games, etc. A visit to the library can also serve as a break for some children.

When you use the timer for on-task behavior, you will set it for different time intervals each time. The first few days, emphasize low time periods and increase the periods as the child demonstrates he or she can stay on task for longer periods. On the first day, you might set the timer for three minutes. If the child stays on task, the next period can be five minutes, then eight, then ten, then jump back to five, then seven, then five, then 12, etc. The main thing is not to set up a pattern that the child can identify. Keep changing the time interval. If the child is successful, you may eventually reach 30-minute or longer periods. Always throw in some shorter (five minute) periods. This style of timing is important to the effectiveness of this approach. Also, your verbal praise is important. When the child is on task, make a big deal of it. Even while the timer is ticking away, give the child feedback ("Tony, you're staying on task, great!")

Group Work

It helps to organize children in groups when teaching them how to pay attention. Groups should consist of three to eight children and should be led by a school counselor or other staff member qualified to organize such a program. Each group meets two or three times a week for one-half hour. During the sessions, the children practice their attending skills. Suggested activities include:

1. Read the group a story. Afterward, ask questions such as "What was the boy's score?" Ask the children to recall facts, names, incidents, etc.
2. Ask the children to repeat number and letter sequences in proper order and backwards (e.g., 1 - L - 7 - 4 - M).
3. Have the children memorize poems, verses, etc.
4. Give the children a math or spelling assignment. Walk around and pass out tokens for children who can stay on task. Make it a contest to see who can earn the most tokens during a specified time (e.g., 20 minutes).

Any activity that requires concentration is valuable. The adult must praise children who respond appropriately. Tokens or tickets are given when children give correct answers or do the right thing. Without such reinforcement, the group approach is ineffective.

Other Suggestions

1. Seat the child in an area having minimal distractions.
2. Give the child a specific time limit to complete an assignment. Encourage the child to gradually increase the amount of time he or she stays on task.
3. Praise the child's completion of a task.
4. Give the child specific rules and always enforce the rules.
5. Let the child tutor or assist children in a younger grade.

Remember, schools can actually turn a hyperactive child into a behaviorally disturbed child. A hyperactive child has some very special needs. By expecting him or her to respond to the school's program as regular children do, without special training, *we* are setting up a problem situation.

Chapter 13

After-School Guidance Activities

My School Wants to have an After-School Hours Guidance Activities Program. How can we do this?

The activities described in this chapter were implemented at a suburban elementary school with a population consisting of 40% Black students, 30% White students, and 30% Hispanic students. Variations of these activities and numerous other activities will meet the needs of populations of other schools. Also, every teacher or counselor feels comfortable conducting activities that are congruent with his or her personality, available time, interest, and physical limitations. This should be a major consideration when you plan an after-school program.

Some of the activities were conducted outside the school building. Your ability to leave school grounds is based on your school system's liability coverage and rules concerning such activities. Some activities involve spending money. Assistance for such expenses may come from the PTA, special fund raising projects, and students paying their share.

Why should my school organize an after-school guidance program?

After-school activities can serve as rewards for accomplishments and improvements during the school day. The busy teacher or counselor may not have the time during the day to devote to all children who need help. Many children cannot be released from the 3 Rs for involvement in such activities.

A child who is socially withdrawn and who has difficulty making friends needs intervention. Parent-school teamwork is essential in any effort to help with a child's total adjustment. Teachers are often restrained in their efforts because one parent or both parents may be working in the daytime and cannot be consulted during the regular school day. Arrangements to confer with parents and organize parent discussion groups will help create positive changes. After-school programs for parents help them learn how to help their children.

If bus transportation for students is not available, and if salary supplements are not available, then some of the activities suggested in this chapter can be carried out during the regular school day.

Sample Activities
Activity 1

Developing Friendships

Objectives
Students exhibiting anti-social behaviors, having negative peer interactions, or generally having difficulty making friends can be involved in action-oriented activities to help reduce the problem. The expected result is an increased awareness of social skills, positive peer experiences, and a reduction of anti-social behaviors.

Student Involvement
One student at a time is the target of the program, but additional class members (three or four) are also involved in the activities.

Materials
Friendship awards, transportation (auto), trip permission forms, snacks, other materials as needed. For activities within the school building, games and playthings are needed.

Facilities
Different facilities may be used at different times (school recreation areas, gyms, public parks, movie theaters, etc.).

Cost
Cost depends on location of activity.

Time
  Approximately 1½ - 2 hours per activity.

Activity Description
  The teacher informs the "friendless" student's class that they are going to do something very exciting. Each day, Billy (the friendless student) will pick a different child in his class who, in his opinion, acted as the best friend to him the whole day.
  At the end of each day, Billy brings his friend of the day to the teacher. The friend receives a friendship certificate. At the end of the week, the best friends that Billy selected all week go on an after-school trip or stay after school for recreational activities.
  The teacher's attitude and excitement should stimulate classmates to make an effort to get to know and be friendly with Billy. The teacher verbally reinforces the friends of the day for being so nice to another person. On the trip (or activity), the teacher reinforces efforts made by Billy to get along with and interact with the other children.

Activity 2

Attendance Motivation

Objective
  To involve students exhibiting attendance problems in school-related activities to increase the attractiveness of school to them and to improve their attendance.

Students Involved
  Approximately six students having poor school attendance.

Materials
  Whatever is needed for the preferred activity.

Facilities
  Classroom, community recreational and educational areas.

Cost
  Cost varies with activity.

Time
  1½ - 2 hours weekly or bi-weekly.

Activity Description

During the school day, students exhibiting attendance problems participate in group and individual counseling, get school jobs and responsibilities, and are made to feel very important in the school.

On a regular basis, these students are invited to participate in special activities after school hours:
- television viewing and games (at school)
- trips
- special projects (e.g., arts and crafts)

Students can participate if they have shown improved attendance.

Activity 3

Community Explorers

Objectives

To provide students with an awareness of the world of work in their community. To share experiences of the community explorers with the entire student body. To supplement and enhance the classroom program in career education.

Student Involvement

Students who have shown improvement in some area are invited to participate.

Materials

Portable cassette tape recorder, camera (optional), transportation.

Facilities

Community work locations (business, professions, labor, etc.).

Cost

Transportation costs.

Time

Approximately 1½ - 2 hours per activity.

Activity Description
During school hours, the community explorers are taught how to interview workers on the job and how to study an occupation.

During the activity a tape recording is made of the workers met by the students. This recording includes the dialogue between the workers and the students. Students are asked to take notes during the visit and prepare an oral presentation for their class.

Each student involved in the activity is asked to participate in a program on the public address system called, *People at Work*. The students discuss their trip and the workers they saw. Special emphasis is put on the need for the number of persons required to operate a particular enterprise. Students are asked to consider jobs they would like for themselves. Sections of the tape recording made during the trip are played over the P.A. system. In addition, each student brings the tape to his or her class and plays the entire recording. Thus, the entire school benefits from the experiences of the community explorers.

Activity 4

Parent Involvement

Objectives
To extend parent consultation hours to the evening when working parents can be contacted, and to extend home visits to the evening when working mothers or both parents may be available for a conference.

Student Involvement
Individual students and families are involved, as necessary.

Materials
None.

Facilities
School's office during the evening or child's home.

Cost
Transportation to homes and school in the evening.

Time
   Amount of time depends on particular needs.

Activity Description
   The teacher or counselor meets with a student's parents in the evening or late afternoon. Conferences are held in the school's office or at the child's home.
   Parent groups, for the purpose of child study or parent effectiveness training, may be conducted in the evening, if parents are available. The advantage is that more fathers are available during evening hours. Such a group should be run by a person trained to run parent study groups.

Activity 5

Clubs

Objective
   To provide special club activities on a short-or long-term basis for students.

Student Involvement
   Select students who will benefit from the activity.

Materials
   As a specific club is formed, proper materials will be needed. For example, the newspaper club needs paper, pencils, mimeo supplies, and a typewriter.

Facilities
   Classroom, guidance room, special area in school, etc.

Cost
   Varies with activity and students' needs.

Time
   Approximately two hours per week per club.

Activity Description
   Special clubs are formed and the leader invites children to participate. Certain target children are picked for club activi-

ties because of the possible therapeutic effects the activities have for them.

One possible club is a newspaper club to produce a monthly school newspaper. Students are trained as reporters. Other possible clubs include a magic club, chess club, photography club, crafts club, and others.

Chapter 14

Improving Standardized Test Performance

How can I Help Children Improve Their Standardized Test Performances?

First, what does available research tell us about test taking?

1. Elementary school children who are taught *how* to take tests show greater gains on testing than students who are not taught how to take tests.
2. Students who receive multiple presentations on how to take a test make greater gains than students who receive single presentations.
3. Test wiseness is an important factor positively affecting test scores.
4. Before they can be successful at test taking, children must understand the concepts of left, right, row, column, most like, and opposite.
5. Test taking motivation varies in different ethnic and socioeconomic groups.
6. Activities immediately preceding a test can affect children's performance. Activities that produce emotional disturbance or fatigue negatively affect the test results.
7. Learning to use relaxation techniques help children perform better on tests.
8. Children's test performance can be improved when the examiner is candid with them about the purposes of testing.
9. Children do better when they are tested in familiar places with familiar company (in the classroom with the classroom teacher).

10. Because guilt and shame often constitute the basis for fear of failure, teachers who do not make children feel shamed during regular class days will have better test performers.
11. Many tests measure a child's ability to skim and his or her eye-hand coordination.
12. Practice testing, when followed by a play period, is a good test taking conditioning method.

I want my students to know how to deal with test questions. What are the basic types of questions most standardized tests have?

Ann Cook of the Community Resources Institute of the City University of New York has spent a long time studying tests. She feels that... "It doesn't matter if it's a test for first graders or graduate students: all standardized tests have four basic types of questions:

"Main Idea Questions ask something like: What is the best title for this paragraph, or what is the author's main point?

"Detail Questions ask for a specific piece of information contained in the preceding paragraph.

"Vocabulary Questions give you a word followed by a set of multiple-choice responses.

"Inference Questions are the most difficult, but you can get a kid to recognize this type immediately by teaching him or her key words and phrases such as: *probably, might, most,* and *likely.*

"The Inference Question will offer choices something like this: Johnny probably loves his mother; doesn't like his mother; wants to kill her. The information is not specifically in the preceding paragraph, but the answer is the one with the word *probably.*

"We teach two fundamental things: First, how to recognize those four types of questions so kids know immediately what they're being asked. Very important. Second, we show them a strategy for each type of test question.

"Take the Detail Question, for example. You teach them to read the answer-choices and then go back and find the appropriate selection in the preceding paragraph. It will be there — practically verbatim — every time, because that's the nature of this type of question.

"With an Inference Question, you teach them to recognize, first, what is being asked and, second, this formula: Based on the information in the paragraph, which answer is most *definitely* true.

"There are questions you teach a kid to ask before taking test, such as: 'Am I penalized for guessing?' If there' penalty, you teach the kid to go through the test and answer carefully all the questions he can and then go back and guess on every remaining one." (Reprinted, with permission, from *The Executive Educator,* Jan., 1977, Vol. 164, Copyright, 1977, *The Executive Educator.* All Rights Reserved.)

> *I understand that children who are taught relaxation techniques often do better on tests. What are some relaxation techniques I can teach my children?*

Relaxation techniques should be taught to children all year and practiced all year. Children should be told to use these techniques to relax during regular classroom tests and assignments, then using relaxation techniques during a testing session will be second nature.

The following relaxation techniques for children are adapted from an article by Arlene Koeppen in the October, 1974 edition of *Elementary School Guidance and Counseling.*

A Relaxation Training Script:
Introduction

> Today we're going to do some special kinds of exercises called "relaxation exercises." These exercises help you learn how to relax when you're feeling uptight and help you get rid of those butterflies-in-your-stomach kinds of feelings. They're also kind of neat, because you can do some of them in the classroom without anybody noticing.
> In order for you to get the best feelings from these exercises, there are some rules you must follow. First, you must do exactly what I say, even if it seems kind of silly. Second, you must try hard to do what I say. Third, you must pay attention to your body. Throughout these exercises, pay attention to how your muscles feel when they are tight and when they are loose and relaxed. And, fourth, you must practice. The more you practice, the more relaxed you can get. Does anyone have any questions?
> Are you ready to begin? Okay. First, get as comfortable as you can in your chair. Sit back, get both feet on the floor, and just let your arms

hang loose. That's fine. Now close your eyes and don't open them until I say to. Remember to follow my instructions very carefully, try hard, and pay attention to your body. Here we go.

Hand and Arms: Pretend you have a whole lemon in your left hand. Now squeeze it hard. Try to squeeze all the juice out. Feel the tightness in your hand and arm as you squeeze. Now drop the lemon. Notice how your muscles feel when they are relaxed. Take another lemon and squeeze it. Try to squeeze this one harder than you did the first one. That's right. Real hard. Now drop your lemon and relax. See how much better your hand and arm feel when they are relaxed. Once again, take a lemon in your left hand and squeeze all the juice out. Don't leave a single drop. Squeeze hard. Good. Now relax and let the lemon fall from your hand. (Repeat the process for the right hand and arm).

Arms and Shoulders: Pretend you are a furry, lazy cat. You want to stretch. Stretch your arms out in front of you. Raise them up high over your head. Way back. Feel the pull in your shoulders. Stretch higher. Now just let your arms drop back to your side. Okay, kittens, let's stretch again. Stretch your arms out in front of you. Raise them over your head. Pull them back. Pull hard. Now let them drop quickly. Good. Notice how your shoulders feel more relaxed. This time let's have a great big stretch. Try to touch the ceiling. Stretch your arms way out in front of you. Raise them way up high over your head. Push them way, way back. Notice the tension and pull harder. Let them drop. You feel relaxed.

Shoulder and Neck: Now pretend you're a turtle. You're sitting out on a rock by a nice, peaceful pond, just relaxing in the warm sun. It feels nice and warm and safe here. Oh-oh! You sense danger. Pull your head into your house. Try to pull your shoulders up to your ears and push your head down into your shoulders. Hold it tight. It isn't easy to be a turtle in a shell. The danger is past now. You can come out into the warm sunshine, and, once again, you can relax and feel the warm sunshine. Watch out now! More danger. Hurry, pull your head back into your house and hold it tight. You have to be closed in tight to protect yourself. Okay, you can relax now. Bring your head out and let your shoulders relax. Notice how much better it feels to be relaxed than to be all tight. One more time, now. Danger! Pull your head in. Push your shoulders way up to your ears and hold tight. Don't let even a tiny piece of your neck and shoulders show outside your shell. Hold it. Feel the tenseness in your neck and shoulders. Okay. You can come out now. It's safe again. Relax and feel comfortable in your safety. There's no more danger. Nothing to worry about. Nothing to be afraid of. You feel good.

Stay as relaxed as you can. Let your whole body go limp and feel all your muscles relax. In a few minutes I will ask you to open your eyes, and that will be the end of this session. As you go through the day, remember how good it feels to be relaxed. Sometimes you have to make yourself tighter before you can be relaxed, just as we did in these exercises. Practice these exercises every day to get more and more relaxed. A good time to practice is at night, after you have gone to bed and the lights are out and you won't be disturbed. It will help you get to sleep. Then, when you are a really good relaxer, you can help yourself relax here at school. Very slowly, now, open your eyes and wiggle your muscles around a little. Very good. You've done a good job. You're going to be a super relaxer. (Copyright 1974 American Personnel and Guidance Association. Reprinted with permission.)

During a break in a testing session, it may be helpful to go through these exercises with children. In addition, encourage them to use these techniques if they feel tense during testing.

When I teach my students how to take a test, what are some things I should include?

You should teach your students:
1. How to pace themselves while taking a test (how much time to spend on each item).
2. How to use computer answer sheets. Make some classroom tests multiple choice tests and use computer answer sheets and scoring services available for teacher-made tests if your school has access to such services.

3. In teaching students how to deal with multiple choice items, show them how two choices can usually be eliminated through logic.
4. When available, use sample tests.
5. Lead discussions before and after testing sessions so that children can express their fears and beliefs about tests.
6. Tell them *not* to make their pencils too sharp. Very sharp pencils break easily and require more time to fill in answer spaces than dull pencils.
7. Encourage children to complete the test during practice testing. Reward students who complete the whole test.
8. Don't get stuck on a difficult item. Go back to it later.
9. Listen to and read directions carefully. During practice testing, ask children to explain the directions to you.

PRACTICE OR SIMULATED TESTING SHOULD RESEMBLE THE REAL THING AND BE OF EQUAL LENGTH TO THE REAL TEST. PRACTICE TEST ITEMS SHOULD NEVER BE BASED ON THE ITEMS OF THE REAL TEST!

10. Show children how to mark their answer sheets using one stroke of the pencil (this can save a lot of time).

What should I tell my students about a particular test they will take?

Tell them:

1. If the test has time penalties and whether a test is scored according to the number of questions answered or according to the number of questions on the test.
2. About the purposes of the testing to be conducted.

A test about testing

Questions:

1. Students should practice how to take standardized tests.
   __X__always _____at times _____never
2. Students should take the risk of guessing if the test does not have a penalty for guessing.
   __X__always _____at times _____never
3. Students should be allowed to complete an untimed test.
   __X__always _____at times _____never

4. After practice testing, students should have a play period.
   __X__ always _____ at times _____ never
5. Tests should be administered to large groups of children in the cafeteria.
   _____ always _____ at times __X__ never
6. It's a good practice for children to take a test right after strenuous physical education.
   _____ always _____ at times __X__ never

Chapter 15

Little Techniques That Work

Tell me About Some Other Ideas for Improving Life at my School

Here are some bits and pieces - little things that can be very effective:

A. Peer Tutoring
B. Parent Study Group
C. Helping Children Learn Decision-Making Techniques
D. Communicating With Kids
E. School-Wide Activities

A. Peer Tutoring
Some children can be effective tutors for other children. Children are probably the greatest untapped resource in our schools. Kids can help each other. There are two ways you can select tutors: age and ability. Age can be a selection factor. You might select a ten-year-old fifth grader to tutor a six-year-old first grader. The fifth grader may be exhibiting a behavior or motivation problem. Perhaps giving this child the opportunity to see what it's like to teach will indirectly have a positive effect on his or her own habits. You can also select tutors by ability. For example, you're a third grade teacher teaching multiplication. Some students have mastered basic multiplication, while others are struggling with it. The students who have mastered the skill can help those who haven't. This can be done for all subject areas including special areas such as art, music, and physical education.

Tutors should have some training in how to help their peers. The following skills can be stressed:

1. Never put down the tutoree (child being tutored). Encourage the tutoree. When he or she gets something right, say something nice to him or her (e.g., "good work," "great," "right on.")
2. If you think the work is too difficult for the tutoree and he or she doesn't understand your explanations, call the teacher for assistance.
3. Don't tell the tutoree the answers. Give him or her a chance to figure it out. If it has taken a lot of time and you see that the tutoree can't figure out the answer, ask, "Would you like me to tell it to you?" Let the tutoree decide if you should provide the answer.

The tutoree's teacher must give the tutor specific directions. These directions must include:

1. The assignment.
2. The tutor's role (listen to reading, teach beginning sound, do samples for tutoree, etc.).
3. When to call the teacher for assistance.
4. Instructional techniques.

If you just put the kids together without a goal for the session and proper supervision, the effectiveness is significantly reduced. The kids are the actors and you're the director, so direct the session. Peer tutoring can have great results. Don't always pick good kids as tutors. Remember, bad kids may become less bad by being in a responsible position and experiencing what it's like to be on the teaching end.

Remember to praise those who do a good job of tutoring. Specific praise about how well they tutor will teach them to be better tutors.

B. Parent Study Group

The most effective way to influence children's development is through their parents. Because parents have the greatest influence on their child's behavior and personality, parent study groups are an effective way to present parents with valid approaches for child rearing.

Several publishers have kits with materials and outlines for running parent study groups. Write to these publishers for their catalogs and perhaps you can select material that would be appropriate for your school.

American Guidance Service
Publisher's Building
Circle Pines, MN 55014

Research Press
2612 North Mattis Avenue
Champaign, IL 61820

Effectiveness Training
   Associates
110 South Euclid Avenue
Pasadena, CA 91101
(offers a national network of training programs for leaders of Parent Effectiveness Training groups.)

H & H Enterprises, Inc.
Box 1070
Lawrence, KS 66044

C. Making Decisions

You can help children learn how to make decisions by teaching them that the decisions they make result in various consequences. These consequences must be accepted and handled. You can show children how they can select alternatives that will result in positive consequences and good feelings. The use of a decision making chart is a simple and effective means of helping children learn how to make decisions.

SAMPLE DECISION MAKING CHART

Problem: Tomorrow is a spelling test. My friend wants me to go with him/her to see a movie tonight, but I need to study my spelling words.

1. Child thinks of his/her alternatives ("Things I can do").
2. Child thinks of what will happen (consequence) if each alternative was acted on.
3. Child considers how each consequence would make him/her feel.
4. Child picks the one alternative on the chart that he/she feels he/she can live with.

ALTERNATIVES	Go to the movie.	Stay home and study spelling.	Get up early and study in the morning.
CONSEQUENCES	I may fail test. Parents might be angry. My friend will be happy.	Good grade. Parents pleased. Friend disappointed.	Probably just pass test. Parents disappointed. Friend happy.
MY FEELINGS IF THIS CONSEQUENCE OCCURS	Angry at myself.	Satisfied and disappointed.	O.K.

Your class can practice using this chart with practice situation such as:

1. You're in the store with your friends. They plan to steal some candy.
2. A kid (your age) tells you that your mother looks like a pig.
3. You are invited to your best friend's birthday party but another friend invites you to go to *(name of an exciting nearby resort area)* for the weekend with his or her family. Both activities occur at the same time).

Children should learn that when they have to make a decision they should say to themselves: "What are the different things I can do?; what will happen if I do each of these things?; how would I feel if this happened?; and which alternative is the best one for me?" During regular classroom activities, remind children to think in these terms as they face having to make a decision.

D. Communicating With Kids
   Take this little test.

1. Do I accept individual opinions without judging them?
   _____ yes   _____ no
2. Do I realize that children may have values different from mine?
   _____ yes   _____ no
3. Do I show children that I genuinely care about their personal and social concerns?
   _____ yes   _____ no
4. Do I refrain from questions which limit the child's thinking (such as "Did you feel happy when it happened?" Better: "How did you feel when it happened?")?
   _____ yes   _____ no
5. Do I establish eye contact when I listen to a child?
   _____ yes   _____ no

Let's go through each of these questions.

1. DO I ACCEPT INDIVIDUAL OPINIONS WITHOUT JUDGING THEM?

Some adults show little, if any, respect for children's opinions, ideas, and feelings when a child expresses an opinion, he or she is immediately cut off.

Poor
Michelle: "The food in the cafeteria is awful!"
Teacher: "Michelle, you should be happy because there are children in other parts of the world who are so hungry that they wish they could eat this lunch."

Better
Michelle: "The food in the cafeteria is awful."
Teacher: "I understand that you dislike our cafeteria food. What is something you can do if you want a better lunch?"

Children can learn to be expressive and to reason only if they are given opportunities to do so. If adults immediately stop children's thoughts from being expressed, the adults are encouraging children to be non-thinkers.

2. DO I REALIZE THAT CHILDREN MAY HAVE VALUES DIFFERENT FROM MINE?

Children's values (feelings, beliefs, things that are important to them) are often rejected by adults. Some values relate directly to the culture of the religion in which the child is raised. For example, a child may live in a neighborhood where fighting is a survival skill. If you teach the child conflict avoidance techniques, you must recognize that some children may not be able to accept such techniques. You can expose them to the techniques so that they will be aware of their alternatives and encourage the use of the techniques at school. When the child leaves school, the decision as to whether or not to use the technique will be his or hers.

You can encourage children to discuss their values and ideas. Teaching in a lecture style is passive for the child and does not require the child to think. Here are some examples that demonstrate how easy it is to encourage children to think and explore their values.

Math: Word problems so that they can lead to exploring feelings and values: Todd has $1.45. His friend asks to borrow 50¢ for an ice cream cone. How much money would Todd have left if he lends the money to his friend? Should Todd lend his friend the money? How do *you* feel when someone wants to borrow something from you?

Science: How do you think Alexander Bell felt when he invented the telephone? Did you ever do anything that made you feel proud or excited?

Which of these inventions would be *most* important in your life? Why?
_____ radio
_____ movie camera
_____ calculator

Vocabulary and Spelling: Include words to increase a child's "feeling" vocabulary (e.g., frustration, excitment, disappointment, etc.).

Physical Education:
a. Tell about the sport you enjoy the most. The least.
b. How do you feel when you're on the winning team? The losing team?

Art: Discuss the moods and feelings of the subjects on a painting. How do you think the painter felt when he or she painted this?

Music: Include songs about self and feelings ("Free to be You and Me," Sesame Street songs, popular music selections). Students should discuss the songs' meanings (in their opinion).

Language Arts: Children can write compositions such as "The Greatest Day in My Life," "My Favorite Things," and "I hate ...."

You can encourage children to express their values and feelings as part of the regular instructional program. Thinking is one of the most important behaviors you can teach.

3. DO I SHOW CHILDREN THAT I GENUINELY CARE ABOUT THEIR PERSONAL AND/OR SOCIAL CONCERNS?

If a child approaches you to express a concern or problem, do you take the time to listen? Just listening to a child shows that child that you care. (See question four below for some related communication techniques.)

4. DO I REFRAIN FROM QUESTIONS THAT LIMIT THE CHILD'S THINKING?

Use open-ended questions if you want to be a good listener and keep communication flowing. You can word questions to give the child an open area in which to respond and the encouragement needed for self-expression, thinking, and self-understanding. Open questions make communication easier and closed questions make communication almost impossible. Here are some examples of open and closed questions.

Open Questions	*Closed Questions*
a. Could you tell me more about that?	Did you then feel bad?

b. How did you feel when that happened? — Did you feel angry?

c. Give me an example. — We can't understand what you mean, talk about something else.

d. What do you do when you get sad? — Do you cry when you're sad?

e. What do you mean when you say your father is out of his mind? — Do you mean your father is in need of psychiatric treatment?

f. What are you feeling as you are telling me this? — I once felt that way too.

5. DO I ESTABLISH EYE CONTACT WHEN I LISTEN TO A CHILD?

The first step in being a good listener is eye contact. *Look* at the child when he or she talks to you. Once you've established eye contact, you're ready for good communications.

6. DO I KNOW THE KEY FACTORS IN LISTENING?

The following are four key factors in listening.

a. *Be Supportive and Avoid Criticism.* Use words and actions that show you care about the child and care about his or her feelings. This will establish, for the child, a feeling of trust toward you. Examples of words and actions that do this are: "Good," "I understand," "Continue," "Tell me more," a pat on the back, eye contact, nodding, and looking interested.

b. *Set a Good Example.* If the child attempts to shock you with a new word or idea, keep calm and don't overreact. If you overreact to a small part of the child's discussion, the child may stop talking and you'll never get to discuss the concern.

c. *Listen to the Child.* Establish eye contact, lean closer, and don't mumble. Let the child know that you know he or she has something important to say.

d. *Repeat Key Ideas.* Mirror back to the child what you hear him or her saying. This really lets the child know that you are listening. It also indicates that you are receiving the same message he or she is sending, and if you're not, then he or she can correct you. Here are some examples of mirror responses:

a. Child: "The coach made me mad when he said I couldn't play."
Teacher: "You are upset because you feel that the coach treated you unfairly.

b. Child: "I wanted to play outside but it's raining! Boy!"
Teacher: "It sounds like you feel disappointed."

When you encourage a child to communicate, you encourage thinking. When you cut off a child's talking, you discourage thinking!

E. School-Wide Activities

Schools can be a dull and boring place. School-wide activities can make children feel more excited about coming to school. Here are a few suggestions for school-wide activities. Use your imagination to create other ideas.

1. *Dress Up Day*. Children come to school dressed for a particular theme.
   a. Western day
   b. Career day (What I want to be when I grow up.)
   c. Circus day
   d. Movie star day
   e. Cartoon character day
   f. President's day
   g. Nations day (Dress in costumes of other nations.)
   h. Famous Americans day

2. *Truck Day*. Put trucks on display for children to view. Contact a variety of businesses (e.g., sanitation, fire, ambulance, cement, moving, ice cream, soft drink, police, etc.) and invite them to display their vehicles. The drivers should be present to explain the use of their vehicles to the children.

3. *Warm Fuzzy Day*. This is a day that everyone pays at least one compliment to someone else.

4. *Career Day*. A variety of people are invited to tell children about their jobs.

5. *Cultural Heritage Day.* Children bring in foods, stories, photos, etc. related to their ancestry.

6. *Mystery Day.* Children are told that something unusual or special is going to happen on a specific date but they have to wait to see what it is. Plan something exciting for the day (e.g., a local TV or radio personality visits the school).

7. *Student Day.* The students run the school. Students assume teacher jobs, custodial, principal, office jobs, etc.

Make your school a place where kids feel wanted and important. This will directly affect their academic success.

Chapter 16

Suggested Readings

Well, you answered a lot of my questions, now what?

If you realize that your responses to children's behavior directly affect their behavior, you are ahead of many persons. Try some of the procedures suggested in this manual. Remember, your enthusiasm for any approach will determine your success in using that approach. You may want to do some additional reading. Here are some suggestions.

Buckley, N.K., and Walker, H.M., *Procedures for School Personnel.* Dryden Press, Elk Grove, IL., 1972.

Dinkmeyer, D., and McKay, G., *Raising A Responsible Child.* Simon & Schuster, New York, 1973.

Dobson, J., *Dare to Discipline.* Tyndale House, Wheaton, IL., 1970.

Glasser, W., *Schools Without Failure.* Harper & Row, New York, 1969.

Kauffman, J., Payne, J., Polloway, E., and Scranton, T. *Living in the Classroom.* Human Sciences Press, New York, 1975.

Krumboltz, J.D., Krumboltz, H.B., *Changing Children's Behavior.* Prentice-Hall, Englewood Cliffs, N.J., 1972.

O'Leary, K.D., and O'Leary, S.G., *Classroom Management: The Successful Use of Behavior Modification.* Maxwell House, Elmsford, N.Y. 10523, 1972.

Sulzer, B. and Mayer, G.R., *Behavior Modification Procedures for School Personnel.* Dryden Press, Elk Grove, IL., 1972.

Walker, H.M., *The Acting-Out Child: Coping with Classroom Disruption.* Allyn & Bacon, Boston, 1979.